THE DAY
Understanding the Most Prophesied Day in the Bible

©2012 by Jim Thomas.
International Standard Book Number: 978-0615724713

Published in association with First Light Ministries.

Scripture quotations taken from the New American Standard Bible®,
Copyright © 1960, 1962, 1963, 1968, 1971, 1972, 1973,
1975, 1977, 1995 by The Lockman Foundation
Used by permission. (www.Lockman.org)

ALL RIGHTS RESERVED

THE DAY

Understanding the Most Prophesied Day in the Bible

JIM THOMAS

To my faithful brothers and sisters of
Living Way Fellowship and The Gathering,

Thanks for enduring with Sherry and I during our growing up years. Many of these revelations I taught in part as the Lord was revealing them to me, but you never had the opportunity to receive the entire teaching. I pray that this work will bless you more than anyone, and guide your preparation for the day.

Many Thanks

I wish to thank my wife for her support and the long hours of enduring, not just the writing of this book, but also the previous ones. You are a saint of God and your reward will be great.

Many thanks also to Kristen, Joy, and Emily who also have sacrificed many hours to help me take this revelation and make it book-worthy.

THE DAY

TABLE OF CONTENTS

PART 1: UNDERSTANDING THE BIBLICAL DAY OF THE LORD

Chapter One: **The Thief is Coming** ... 6
Chapter Two: **Twenty-four Hours or a Thousand Years?** ... 14

PART 2: THE DAY OF THE LORD—THE DAY OF JUDGMENT

Chapter Three: **The Season of Warnings** ... 26
Chapter Four: **The Terrible Day of the Lord** ... 34
Chapter Five: **Day Two The Rise of Antichrist** ... 50
Chapter Six: **The Time of Jacob's Trouble** ... 67

PART 3: THE DAY OF THE LORD—THE DAY OF HIS RETURN

Chapter Seven: **The Marriage Supper of the Lamb** ... 76
Chapter Eight: **Revealing Messiah** ... 85

PART 4: THE DAY OF THE LORD—JESUS' RULE AND REIGN

Chapter Nine: **The Throne of Jesus—Ezekiel's Temple** ... 94
Chapter Ten: **The Judgment Seat of Christ— The Reward of the Saints** ... 102
Chapter Eleven: **Israel's Glory and Prince David** ... 111
Chapter Twelve: **The Restored Earth— Rebuilding the Ruins** ... 120
Chapter Thirteen: **Satan's Final Stand** ... 128

PART 5: PREPARING FOR THE DAY OF THE LORD

Chapter Fourteen: **This Generation** ... 138
Chapter Fifteen: **Preparing for the Day** ... 149

The Ten Undeniable Facts of the Day of the Lord ... 164

About the Author ... 167

THE DAY

PREFACE

I wanted to write this book for many years; there are many reasons why I waited until now. First, I wanted to be sure that I saw the day of the Lord as clearly as I could; so I waited for the Lord's permission and His anointing. I didn't begin until the Lord dropped the outline into my spirit, and until I sensed it was my divine assignment from Him.

To be honest, I kept waiting for this revelation to be given to Bible teachers who are much more influential than I. The church is in desperate need of awakening to the lateness of the hour, and to understand that what is prophesied will soon come upon us. I don't know who will listen to this country shepherd from Southwest Pennsylvania, but I can no longer contain the burden that I have for the church to be prepared for the difficult times that lie ahead. I had to write this book.

There have been many books written on the end times; most are written with the center of focus around the church's departure, or rapture. Many never mention the most prophesied day of the Bible. As the birth pangs continue to warn us of its certain coming, it is time for the church to wake up from its slumber and ignorance about this day, and join the Thessalonians, who would never be unprepared for its coming, even though it arrives suddenly.

Let me warn the reader now. There are no predictions of when this day arrives, or of the day of Christ's certain return. It is time to realize that none of us knows the hour of its arrival, yet we must heed Joel's warning that its coming is near.

This book endeavors to be an in-depth Bible study of the

day of the Lord, and all of its different days and seasons. It is an attempt to warn the church and the world, if it will listen, of the most difficult time that any generation has ever faced or ever will have to face. Jesus and all of the prophets saw this day coming and warned us of the devastating judgment that must precede the Lord's return.

Because of the language of the prophets and their use of the word "day" in their messages, there is much confusion over this great day that is very, very near. My hope and prayer is that this teaching will help alleviate this confusion and make another prophetic cry for believers to prepare themselves for the judgment that is soon to encompass the earth.

Most believers are fixed on their belief that the rapture will take place before the judgment, so they don't have to think about being here during the dark, dark night. It is time to rethink this position, for it was this same type of thinking that led the foolish virgins not to prepare adequately. They didn't gather enough oil, and the bridegroom came much later than they expected.

The end time focus of the Bible is not on the rapture of the church, but on the coming of the Lord. It is His day, not ours. His day is to bring judgment on the rebellious and unbelieving, repaying the world for the treatment of the ones whom He sent to them. In His day, the times of the Gentiles will be fulfilled; He will begin to exterminate sinners from the earth, while miraculously saving Israel for her final destiny. Jesus will return to earth on His day and vanquish the armies of this world, as well as the antichrist. In His day, He will set up His rule and His reign in Jerusalem and usher in an unprecedented time of peace and joy. Every knee will bow and every tongue will confess that Jesus Christ is Lord when He reigns in His day.

It is time for us to focus on His day and leave the timing of our gathering together in God's hands. It is time to heed Jesus' own warnings about the coming of His day. It is also time to revisit the prophets, who saw this day coming thousands of years ago and prophesied its arrival. Every believer should be like the Thessalonians, who were well aware of the coming of this day and were prepared for the great upheaval – the removal of this antiquated Babylonian system and the establishment of Jesus' rule and reign upon this earth. It truly is a great and terrible day that is drawing near.

THE DAY

PART 1:

UNDERSTANDING THE BIBLICAL DAY OF THE LORD

Chapter One
THE THIEF IS COMING

I Thessalonians 5:2 – "For you yourselves know full well that the day of the Lord will come just like a thief in the night."

The most prophesied day in the Bible is drawing near, very near as the prophet Joel warned us. There is a thief coming, and when he comes, it will be the beginning of a long, long night. His coming is ordained of the Lord and so is his mission. He will destroy Babylon the Great.

This thief will pilfer the world. His mission will be to strip the earth of all its luxuries and its idyllic tendencies to love silver, gold, metal, and wood. Most modern day conveniences will be stolen and destroyed by this thief. A generation, who has put much emphasis on stocks and bonds, luxurious houses, stylish clothing, automobiles, and every electronic device known to man, is being fattened in the day of slaughter (James 5:1-6). The thief is coming.

Ahead of his coming, it still looks like the Garden of Eden, but behind his devastating march is a desolate wilderness. He is quicker than a fire burning out of control, and nothing can stand against his advance. When he is through, the land will be stripped, as if hungry locusts had devoured it. The thief is coming (Joel 2:1-11).

Who is this thief? His name is Judgment. He has been held back and prepared for the exact day and hour of his appearing. When he is unleashed, the earth will literally totter. He will come with many facets of devastation and with many targets for his wrath. When he arrives, he will be absolutely relentless about his mission. His purpose is to exterminate sinners from the face of the earth (Isaiah 13:9-13).

No amount of prayers will stop his agenda, for he is the answer to the many prayers of suffering saints. The bowl, which judgment is poured out of in heaven, appears to be the very same bowl that contained the intercessions and the precious prayers of saints. The bowl is filled to overflowing and will soon be poured out (Revelation 5:8 and Revelation 16).

The Thief is Just

Righteous and True are also his names. He is not unfair in his dealings, though the world will hardly see it that way. Babylon has no idea how she has mistreated the righteous and scorned the prophets sent to her. She has discounted them all and even had many of them put to death; her garments are stained in blood and her judgment was foretold long ago.

The thief is coming. He is a forerunner, one who is to clear the way of the soon coming King. His edicts are righteous; his ways are just. The prophets saw him coming and proclaimed his day. They sounded the alarm and warned of his complete devastation and of his holy march. He will not stop until he accomplishes what he is sent to do (Joel 2:1-11).

Babylon is his target, and her tentacles have spread throughout all the earth. Her glamorous, immoral ways will be brought to an end; her idols will be destroyed. All of her financial systems will melt down and vanish. Her kingdoms, cities, her politics, and religions will be no more. All who are in love with her will have a face-to-face encounter with this thief.

Sadly, much of what is called the church has been caught in Babylon's deceiving web. This church is in love with this present world and has given in to its pressures. In the Bible, the unfaithful church is called the harlot. Her garments are blood stained from the persecution of many of the apostles and prophets sent to her. She has forsaken her Husband and become completely entangled in worldly affairs. The gold and the silver she has coveted will not deliver her on the day when the thief comes. When Babylon is destroyed, the harlot will also be destroyed (Revelation 17).

But, he hasn't come, not yet. There is still time to repent and amend our ways. When Joel was given a vision of the judgment, he proclaimed the need for fasting and a solemn assembly. It is time for our leaders to lead this solemn assembly with weeping and repentance, crying out and calling on the name of the Lord. It is time to proclaim His Lordship, before the thief comes and proclaims it for us. We cannot stop his coming, but we don't have to be his target.

STAY AWAKE!

It is time to wake from our perilous sleep, to stop pretending we don't know that this thief is coming. The New Testament continually warns us against falling asleep in the last days. We are drowsy from anesthesia, but we must wake up. The day that is about to dawn is the most prophesied day in the Bible. Every believer, who has a Bible and opens the pages to read, can know of the thief's impending arrival.

Yet so much of the preaching today is like anesthesia before the slaughter. We have fulfilled Paul's prophetic admonition that we would gather for ourselves teachers who would tickle our ears. They are putting us to sleep and are afraid to challenge us with truth. We are sleeping, but we must wake up! There is still so much to do, and so little time to do it.

The purpose of this book is to unashamedly examine and proclaim the coming day of the Lord. Despite the quantity of information in the Bible about this day, very little teaching about it is available in the church. It is inconceivable that we could be so close to the day of the Lord and still be unaware of its coming impact.

Jesus warned us to stay alert during the season of His soon return. The Bible calls these times perilous. We live during the most dangerous of all times to be alive on the earth, for the capability of nations to destroy this world is beyond our comprehension. Yet it is also the most luxurious of all times to be alive. People are so enamored with their idols that they don't even realize their lives and lifestyles are hanging by a thread. The thief is coming.

As believers, we should be preparing ourselves and our loved ones for the day of the Lord. Perhaps He will choose to snatch us away before the thief comes. Even so, should we not care enough for our neighbors and unbelieving loved ones to warn them of the coming judgment? What if the Lord tarries and chooses to leave us here during the time of the great tribulation? What if our only hope is the protection of our righteous relationship with Jesus? It is time to wake up!

Are we ready to go through the most difficult time the world has ever known, in a world ruled by an antichrist and devastated by the judgments which God is pouring out? Can this fast-food, microwaving, electronic-loving generation make it in a world where surviving the next day is its only goal?

Jesus told us that the days of this thief's pilfering would be shortened so that the elect could be saved. "And if it is with difficulty that the righteous is saved, what will become of the godless man and the sinner (I Peter 4:18)?" The days of judgment that lie ahead are the most difficult mankind will ever face.

Early or Late Gathering?

None of us know the time when believers will be gathered together unto the Lord. Both theories of an early and late gathering are possible. Even Jesus didn't seem to know whether He would come early or late. He told us to prepare ourselves for both scenarios. Whenever He comes, we are to be ready.

Jesus' warned us to stay alert and be on guard for the thief who is coming. Could it be that people who are set on the early rapture of the church are like the foolish virgins who didn't gather enough oil for their lamps? In this sobering parable in Matthew 25, Jesus warned us of the possibility of His late arrival. They weren't prepared to meet the Bridegroom when He came much later than they expected.

Years ago, I was a high school basketball coach. Youth have a tendency to see easy opponents on their schedule and prepare sloppily for the game, convinced they won't have any trouble beating those teams. A coach should always over-prepare his team and never let them develop lazy and sloppy habits that are a cancer to a team. When a coach prepares his team for an onslaught, for the best that another team can bring, then the game will actually be easier than practice. Young people will learn lessons of life and be grateful for the preparation.

What happens if you under-prepare a team for a game? The team will eventually get ambushed. They will lose to a team that they should have beaten.

Why do we prepare our churches for the easiest of all scenarios? Should we not prepare them for the battle, so that we can face the long night and still be victorious? Any wise leader can see this ambush coming.

If I over-prepare someone, and then, the real thing is easier than the preparation, I have done my job as a leader. What if I do the opposite and teach an early departure, when in fact, Jesus returns late? What will the Lord do to me for allowing such sloppy preparation?

We don't know the hour of our gathering to Him. Every one who has set a date and declared a time has been proven to be a false prophet and has blemished the end time's mission of the church. Unfortunately, we probably haven't seen the last of their false predictions. The message of the early rapture is attractive to the flesh – we all want to believe that we won't have to face severe tribulation.

ONE COMING OR TWO?

The Bible only refers to the coming of the Lord; it is speculation to believe in two comings of Jesus. In the "two comings" theology, Jesus first returns, only for His bride. He will come and get her before (what most believe), or in the middle of (the minority opinion), the tribulation. Later, the bride of Christ returns with Him at the end of the tribulation, thus completing the two comings of Jesus. I respect these believers for warning us to be ready at any moment to leave this world behind and cling to our Savior. But they are only declaring half of the message.

Jesus told us to be ready for His late arrival as well. In this theology, the rapture and the second coming occur on the same day and happen at the same time, thus just one return of the Lord. The purpose of our gathering together unto Him is to join the army of heaven in the return of our Lord. This book will be written from that perspective, not because I am absolutely convinced that it is the right perspective, but because it prepares the church to endure and hold fast to our testimony during the perilous times that are certain to come. It also motivates us to read the Bible, to be more aware of the thief who is coming, and to prepare ourselves for his arrival.

We must stop discounting the pages and pages of truth written in the Bible because of our excuse that we won't be here when these terrible judgments occur. The time is late, and it is imperative that we put off lazy Christianity and sloppy Bible study. The Lord told us explicitly of this day. He wants us to anticipate its coming.

Preparing for the Harvest

Not all of our training and preparation is for the hard times. We must also prepare for a great harvest of souls who will come into the kingdom during the end times. Daniel saw this day and said, "Those who have insight among the people will give understanding to the many; yet they will fall by sword and by flame, by captivity and plunder for many days." (Daniel 11:33) It will not be easy to live during these times, but a great harvest of souls will be gathered in the end.

Preparedness is always the key to taking action. "But the people who know their God will display strength and take action (Daniel 11:32)." Believers must be aware of the judgment in order to prepare for its impact. We must also be ready to harvest during a very difficult time. "Those who have insight will shine brightly like the brightness of the expanse of heaven, and those who lead the many to righteousness, like the stars forever and ever (Daniel 12:3)." Armed with the oil of preparation, the "wise virgins" of our day will shine brightly and lead many to righteousness.

Jesus stated that the tribulation would come upon all who are on the earth. We must cleanse ourselves of every Babylonian lust and warn those who are still trapped in her lairs. Our Lord is looking for a bride adorned with righteous acts and prepared for His arrival. It is our time to shine, for it is also our generation that is being prepared for the slaughter. We must warn them of the things that will shortly take place on this earth.

Chapter Two

TWENTY-FOUR HOURS OR A THOUSAND YEARS?

II Peter 3:8 – "But do not let this one fact escape your notice, beloved, that with the Lord one day is like a thousand years and a thousand years like one day."

It **is impossible to understand the day of the Lord without consulting the prophets.**

The declarations of the prophets are some of the most difficult passages of scripture to understand. Most believers avoid this section of the Bible because they believe that it is too hard to comprehend. Yet, within these pages are found the most astonishing predictions of events that would take place many years to follow. And many of them are still waiting to be fulfilled.

Prophetic Truths

There are several truths that we must keep in mind when studying the prophets. First, as Peter would state years later, all prophecy was given by God and was inspired by the Holy Spirit. The prophets are just as important and inspired as the rest of scripture. Yet it has been my experience that they are the least read and the least understood part of the Bible.

It is within their messages that the day of the Lord is proclaimed. Inspired Word isn't always easy to understand. God spoke exactly what He wanted to communicate, but often these truths are hidden in lengthy discourses that may even have applied to another king or time.

Another truth about prophecy is that it reveals the past as well as the present and the future. Roots and foundations are often mentioned in the prophets. For instance, how many times did the prophets refer to the nation of Israel and call her Jacob? Hosea referred to the Northern Kingdom as Ephraim; Obadiah calls Edom, Esau. The prophets constantly refer to the roots of nations and often to the very character of the person that founded the nation. Many times the nation keeps repeating the same character flaws of the original founder.

Satan's fall from grace was revealed through prophecy, but exposed through the rebellion of kings and nations. In Isaiah 14, Satan's original rebellion is revealed through a prophecy directed to the king of Babylon, and in Ezekiel 28, his fall is exposed even more through a prophecy directed at the king of Tyre.

In order to understand prophecy, one must have a good grasp of the history and events that happened earlier. Prophecy doesn't just reveal the mysteries of the future but also the mysteries of the past.

This brings us to another crucial truth for understanding the prophets. Prophecies are rarely chronological and often go forward or backward in time within the span of a few verses. Prophecies are literally timeless. God speaks as if a thousand-year old event just happened, or as though an event that will happen in the distant future is happening now. This further shrouds the prophecies in mystery.

We must ask several questions. Why does God do that to us?

Doesn't He know that we are chronological people, that we like order and clarity? Why then do prophecies go backward, then forward, or forward then backward? Why does all of it seem like it is ready to happen at the moment it is pronounced? How do we discern between the present revealed word, the past foundations, and the future fulfillment?

Many times we don't have to. The prophecies of past and future are often one and the same. Listen to a wise king of Israel who understood this truth. "That which is has been already, and that which will be has already been, for God seeks what has passed by (Eccl. 3:15)." Prophecies are timeless and keep repeating themselves over again.

Prophecy helps us to understand God's perspective. God's view of time is so different than ours. That is why He can reveal something that happened thousands of years ago and make it seem like it was just yesterday. He also has shown the prophets events that will happen thousands of years in the future, but from the prophet's perspective, it seems so close that they warn, "Near!" Prophecies about the Lord's first and second comings are intertwined because from God's perspective, they are only a short time apart and are actually a part of the same day.

Remember being a child and agonizing over how long it would be until the next Christmas? Doesn't our perspective of time change as we mature? Imagine being the Ancient of Days! Perhaps we can understand why His perspective is different than ours.

REPEATING FOUNDATIONS

It is very important that we understand the foundations, since they inevitably keep repeating throughout history. Israel is one of those foundations. Many believers today apply prophetic scriptures to themselves or their circumstances because they believe that Israel represents the people of God or all the people of faith. Therefore, as God spoke to Israel, so He speaks to us today.

Babylon is another one of those foundations that has been fulfilled again and again throughout the history of man. Babylon is not just the location on earth where the original country existed; it is the root and the foundation of all nations – the way they think, grasp for power, and protect their boundaries.

It was in Babylon that God divided the language of the people and scattered them, where they eventually gathered into the various nations of the world. Roots of rebellion, schisms, and territorial wars all began to form, and much of history has repeated these same battles. The race was on, with every nation of this world trying to be the greatest, paranoid of the advances of other nations. Nations still war with each other and treat each other with contempt because of their Babylonian roots.

Babylon is also the birthplace of religion. It was there that man began to build towers or temples, trying to reach to heaven. Religion's main goal is to find God and make man acceptable to get to heaven. Religion offers a pathway, rituals, or a set of beliefs with the aim to please God and take man to heaven. Out of Babylon, every religion that exists today has its roots. In Babylon, man began to worship and bow down to gods and idols of his own making and of his own understanding.

Though religion has the best intentions, it is the great deception. Man can never make himself good enough to get to heaven. No amount of rituals, right doctrine, or good moral values will ever be enough to reach to God; God must reach down to us. Religion always poses a distant god. Christianity reveals a relationship to a very personal God who loves us and gave Himself up for us.

Religion is the most divisive of all entities. It has probably caused as many wars as national conflicts have. The roots of religion are the same as the roots of nations – all of them return back to this mystery of Babylon.

The target of the end times is this Babylon. Don't look for a nation to form in the Middle East or mistakenly refer to Iraq as that place. The original Babylon was located within the borders of Iraq thousands of years ago, but it was destroyed and is now a desert. Since then, many other strong nations and religions – usually the mix of the two – have risen out of these roots and fulfilled again the prophecies of Babylon. Once you know the foundations and roots of Babylon, you will see her fulfillment throughout history and also in your own time.

The judgment of the end times is coming upon this Babylon. Babylon the Great consists of all the nations of the world, their economies, and their religions. They all owe their roots to this original giant. All of them have set up their own rule and oppose the rule of Jesus. Jesus said that His followers would be hated by all nations during the season before He will return to earth.

Understanding the Word "Day"

In order to understand more clearly the day of the Lord, we must also understand the use of the word "day" in the prophecies. For the most part, the word day in the Bible refers to a twenty-four hour time period. Any argument that it took God six thousand years to create the world instead of six twenty-four hour days is ridiculous. When the Bible talks about evening and morning, it is referring to one twenty-four hour day. We must be careful how we use the word "day" and how we apply its different meanings.

The word "day" can, however, also refer to a season. Some of the favorite uses of it by the prophets are prophecies that start out, "And in that day." Many of the prophecies of the Lord's rule and reign on the earth begin with this phrase. This is not a direct measure of time, but refers to another season or epoch that is different from the present "day."

It is evident in the prophets that Christ's first appearance on the earth, His substitutionary death, His resurrection, ascension, and the formation of the church were the beginnings of the "day of the Lord." It is also evident that the entire thousand-year rule and reign of Christ and the preceding judgment that occurs happen in this "day." Sometimes, just the judgment is declared to be the "day of the Lord." Several prophecies refer singly to the first day of that judgment, and it is also called the day of the Lord.

Significant Twenty-four Hour Days in the Day of the Lord

There are a few twenty-four hour days of significance in the season of the day of the Lord. These significant days are highlighted in the Old Testament with a corresponding feast. The spring feasts were fulfilled in Jesus' first coming and the fall feasts will be fulfilled in His return.

The first very significant day in the day of the Lord is the Passover, or the day that Jesus was crucified on the cross. This day, our salvation was purchased as the blood of the unblemished Lamb of God was applied to the doorposts of our lives.

The entire gospel is centered on this event. Without Jesus' substitutionary death, nobody would have been spared the punishment of eternal damnation. Christ's body lay in the grave during the feast of the Unleavened Bread, and He rose on the feast of the First Fruits.

Fifty days after Jesus' resurrection, at the feast of Pentecost, the Spirit was poured out, and the Lord formed His church and breathed life and power into her. At that time, Peter quoted a day of the Lord passage from Joel 2 and told the people that this scripture was being fulfilled this day.

On the day of Pentecost, Jesus confronted the Babylonian curse of the divisive languages that had caused the original split. People from many countries who spoke different languages all heard the gospel preached to them in their own language. Out of these roots, the church was formed to reach the nations of the earth. The spring feasts of Passover and Pentecost are twenty-four hour days that have had great significance in our history and have already been fulfilled in the day of the Lord.

There are more to come. The prophets often refer to the first day of the horrific judgment as "the day of the Lord." Another very significant day will be the return of Christ and the final judgment on the nations in the Valley of Armageddon. This day will end the season of judgment that is between these two days.

As the prophets saw each of these days from a distance, they called each one the "day of the Lord." Each day accomplishes a purpose bringing Christ's kingdom to the earth. Therefore, there are many prophecies about this day, some very frightening, and some that are very exciting. All of them comprise the great and terrible day of the Lord.

Defining the Day of the Lord

So then, what is this great and terrible day of the Lord? It is the time that the Lord has fixed in eternity to judge the Babylonian system, which we have been living under for several thousands of years, and to restore His kingdom to the earth. He accomplished the beginning of this with His first appearance, atoning death, and powerful resurrection; He will finish it at His second coming with His literal rule on the earth. All who have believed the gospel and received His Lordship are welcomed into His kingdom as His messengers who herald His soon return.

The terrible day of the Lord is a fixed day that is soon to arrive. On that day, judgment will be released on the nations in preparation for the return of Jesus. This day will also begin the time of Jacob's trouble. It will be a short season of tribulation and continued judgment on sinners who have never received the Lordship of Jesus.

Following this terrible season of judgment, comes another fixed day set by the Father. This is the great day of the Lord when Jesus will return and under His rule and reign, the earth will be restored. The knowledge of the Lord will cover the earth as the waters cover the sea. Governing cities and ruling the nations under His direct oversight from Jerusalem is the reward for those who believed in Him and received His Lordship during the prior Babylonian age.

Where are we in this timeline in history? Israel has been a nation for over sixty years, and the time of the Gentiles is coming to an end. The next great moment of history belongs to the thief who will come on the terrible day of the Lord. We are being warned by the birth pangs of judgment, which are already upon us with consistent regularity.

As I write this book, one of the most devastating droughts in our nation's history is upon us. Warning after warning has come from the merciful hand of the Lord. What is He warning? The time for Babylon the Great to be judged is here, and all the earth is about to experience the thief in the night.

Is the day of the Lord a twenty-four hour day or a seasonal period that is about a thousand years in length? The answer to both questions is yes. The significant twenty-four hour days are called the day of the Lord; so is the entire season of the fulfillment of Christ's kingdom coming to this earth. Let's go on now to examine the season that the Bible declares we are currently in, and the prophetic events that are soon to take place, already revealed in the prophets. Though we don't know that day or the hour of their arrival, we can know with certainty the season we are now living in and the judgments that will soon shake the earth. Knowing the fear of the Lord, we must warn men.

Twenty-four Hours or a Thousand Years?

THE DAY

PART 2:

THE DAY OF THE LORD— THE DAY OF JUDGMENT

Chapter Three
THE SEASON OF WARNINGS

Luke 21:25 – "There will be signs in sun, and moon, and stars, and on the earth dismay among nations, in perplexity at the roaring of the seas."

Preceding the release of the thief will be a time of warning, as the Lord in His mercy calls to the earth before the Day of Judgment. Jesus had the clearest vision of this season of warning and told us plainly that it would come as a precursor to the Great Tribulation. Each birth pang, in and of itself, is a small judgment that often takes lives and warns the living of the coming season of judgment.

How will we know when this warning season is upon us? It won't be easy to discern if you listen to the world. Peter warns us that mockers will proclaim that all continues just as it was from the beginning of creation. (II Peter 3:4) They will argue that these same events have always taken place throughout history, and that there is nothing special about our time. Peter made it very clear that history is moving to a climatic end. Jesus prophesied that we would know the season of His soon arrival and the warnings that would come preceding the judgment of the day of the Lord.

The Fig Tree

Jesus told His disciples a parable to help them discern the times and the seasons. "Behold the fig tree and all the trees, as soon as they put forth leaves, you see it and know for yourselves that summer is near (Luke 21:29-30)." What does this fig tree represent?

Jesus is alluding to the nation of Israel. The prophets used the fig tree several times to illustrate Israel's plight. Jeremiah saw a vision from the Lord about good and bad figs. They represented the children of Israel, those who were obedient and those who weren't.

Just days prior to this conversation with his disciples, Jesus cursed a fig tree for being fruitless. It withered and died by the next morning. Again, this fig tree represented Israel, her fruitlessness, and her impending judgment. It was a sign of the judgment on Jerusalem and on the nation of Israel shortly after His departure. In A.D. 70, both Israel and Jerusalem were destroyed and have since been trampled underfoot by the Gentiles – exactly what Jesus prophesied would happen.

Israel did not exist as a nation again until 1948, and Jerusalem didn't come under Israeli control until 1967. Since then, Israel has risen rapidly to power because of her friendship with the United States of America. Since the 1990's, many Jews from behind the iron curtain have returned to their homeland. Israel has been established as a nation – the fig tree has now put forth its leaves. Summer is near. Therefore, the season of warnings is upon us.

Birth Pangs

Jesus offers us a great analogy when He refers to the warnings as "birth pangs." He compares the season of warnings to the process of birthing a child. His kingdom has been hidden and opposed by the unbelieving and the immoral, though it has been experienced by those of us who believe. This kingdom of His rule and reign is about to be birthed physically on the earth. The earth meanwhile groans, like an expectant mother, waiting for the revelation of the sons of God. The King, rejected at His first coming, will return and establish His kingdom on earth. The earth is preparing for the birth of the coming kingdom.

The warnings are called birth pangs for another reason. Birth pangs come and go, increase and then subside. That is the nature of birth pangs. So it is during this season, as several events each year warn us of the judgment that is right outside our door.

For example, we have witnessed the onslaught of AIDS, which has killed over one million people. It is one of the pestilences that the apostle John saw in his prophecy in the book of Revelation. We also have witnessed wars and rumors of wars, droughts and famines, earthquakes, and nature's wrathful storms, all of which have taken a major toll on life in various places of the world – again, fulfilling exactly what Jesus said would happen. We have experienced a multitude of warnings already, but the frequency of them still remains fairly slow and inconsistent. It is still easy to explain them all away.

Very soon, the intensity and the frequency will increase. How do I know? I just asked my wife. Birth pangs become much more intense and much more frequent as the time to give birth arrives. When our sons were born, my wife reached a time when she had little rest before another round of intense pain and pressure started again

So it will be on this earth, and there is nothing we can do to stop it – just like there is nothing a woman can do to prevent giving birth when the time is upon her. Jesus wants us to recognize what time it is and to look upward to Him, for our redemption is drawing very near. He is doing this for those of us who believe in Him.

Revelation gives us a look at this season with the opening of the seals in Revelation 6. This prophetic book is written in an apocalyptic style, and as a result, it often is the most unread and least understood part of the New Testament. Revelation is a prophetic word, and, like the prophets, is not written with strict chronological order. Instead, Jesus gives us pictures and images of the day of the Lord, in a message that is full of Old Testament imagery.

The "horsemen of the apocalypse" (as they are often described) represent ways the Lord will judge the earth during this season of warning. War, famine, pestilence, and death have been released on this earth as a warning that the judgment of Babylon is beginning. We have already witnessed such judgments. In recent years, a flood has devastated the city of New Orleans after Hurricane Katrina. A tsunami has killed tens of thousands in Asia, and an earthquake humbled the entire nation of Japan. There are more birth pangs to come, with even more catastrophic results. It can be frightening to us if we don't understand that all of this is being done for us who believe.

The Lord is setting in motion His plan to rescue us from a world tarnished by sin and given over to immorality and idols of every kind. Just as He did in Egypt thousands of years ago, God began the deliverance of His people with prophetic warnings that got progressively harder on the Egyptians. So it is again, but this time all nations will be judged – not just Egypt. The birth pangs have been spread out over the entire world.

This makes them harder to recognize, since many of them don't directly affect us.

Nations in Dismay

Recently, many nations have struggled with looming economic problems and uprisings against their central governments. This is another sign of the coming judgment. Not only did Jesus predict this, but so did the second Psalm and Isaiah 34.

"Why are the nations in an uproar and the peoples devising a vain thing? The kings of the earth take their stand and the rulers counsel together against the Lord and against His anointed." (Psalm 2:1-2) All the problems that nations face today are the result of their stubborn refusal to acknowledge Jesus as Lord. Instead, world leaders are taking their stand and counseling together to figure out how to stay in control. But the world is shaking, and the problems are becoming insurmountable.

"He who sits in the heavens laughs, the Lord scoffs at them. Then He will speak to them in His anger and terrify them in His fury saying, 'But as for Me, I have installed My King upon Zion, My holy mountain." (Psalm 2:4-6) The judgment of nations has begun and the time to declare the Lordship of Christ is now. He is the only answer for the plight of nations. However, they will not bow their knee to Him just yet.

"Now therefore O kings, show discernment; take warning O judges of the earth. Worship the Lord with reverence and rejoice with trembling. Do homage to the Son, that He not be angry, and you perish in the way, for His wrath may soon be kindled. How blessed are all who take refuge in Him!" (Psalm 2:10-12) There is only one safe place on earth during these perilous times. We must find our refuge in Jesus.

The nations are in turmoil, and we have only just begun to see the effects. I wonder as I write this book what will become of Syria? Will Damascus be destroyed now or later, as Isaiah 17 predicts it will? I watch these world events with a newspaper in my hands and a Bible in my lap. We must realize what has already been written will shortly take place.

When I was very young, I watched a show on television called *Lost in Space*. There was a robot on the show whose job was to warn the lost family of impending danger that it could sense before they could. "Warning, warning, warning," the robot cried anytime danger was near.

It is the job of the preacher and the messengers of the kingdom to sound the alarm and warn people of the impending danger that is coming; they are not aware of it. These warnings may seem to go unnoticed. I really don't remember much about the show, *Lost in Space*. But, forty-five years later, I can still hear that silly robot say, "Warning, warning, warning." The warnings of the Lord will stay with the people we warn. Some may receive them now; some may receive them later. Either way we have a job to do, as we add our voices to the birth pangs happening all over the world.

"Jesus, the Lord, is coming! Receive His Lordship now! Do not put your trust in silver or gold, or in your nation's ability to protect and save you! Jesus is bringing every nation to its knees. One day, every knee will bow and every tongue will confess that Jesus is Lord!" The only safe refuge during these times is a life hidden in Christ.

I pray that the Lord will give us the boldness to warn our generation of the impending judgment. The Lord has placed each one of us in a strategic place to sound the alarm and be witnesses of His wonderful rule in His kingdom. It is such a blessing to be safe under the wings of the Almighty and in His shelter. Let us pray that many more will find refuge in Him. We will all need His shelter in the days to come.

Listen to the scriptures that are warning us and prepare us to warn others. The season of warning is upon us now!

> "Blow a trumpet in Zion, and sound the alarm in My holy mountain. Let the inhabitants of the land tremble, for the day of the Lord is coming; surely it is near." (Joel 2:1-2).

> "Gather yourselves together, yes, gather, O nation without shame, before the decree takes effect – that day passes like the chaff – before the burning anger of the Lord comes upon you, before the day of the Lord's anger comes upon you. Seek the Lord, all you humble of the earth who have carried out His ordinances; seek righteousness, seek humility. Perhaps you will be hidden in the day of the Lord's anger." (Zephaniah 2:1-3)

> "Consecrate a fast, proclaim a solemn assembly; gather the elders and all the inhabitants of the land to the house of the Lord your God, and cry out to the Lord. Alas for the day of the Lord is near, and it will come as destruction from the Almighty." (Joel 1:14-15)

The sons of Issachar understood the times and the seasons that they were living in and were able to give wise counsel to the people. I pray that this generation in the church would awake from its slumber to proclaim the times that are upon us.

It is evident why there are so many warnings in the Bible about falling asleep in the last days. Perhaps we have been warned so much about the end times that we are becoming immune to them. How can it be that we are this close to the most devastating time on earth, and even the church isn't aware of it? We must wake up and warn our generation of the coming day of the Lord.

We are now experiencing the warnings of the birth pangs of judgment. Nations are in an uproar, and we can only pray that there is still more time left in this season of warning. Eventually, the season of warnings will intensify and then end. The terrible day of the Lord will be upon us.

Chapter Four
THE TERRIBLE DAY OF THE LORD

Jeremiah 25:33 – "Those slain by the Lord on that day will be from one end of the earth to the other. They will not be lamented, gathered or buried; they will be like dung on the face of the ground."

The day the thief is released is often called the "day of the Lord." Most of the prophets got a glimpse of this day and wrote about it in their discourses. Isaiah, Jeremiah, Ezekiel, Joel, Amos, Zephaniah, and Zechariah all tried to describe it. The apostle John saw this day and wrote about it in apocalyptic imagery.

If you have never studied this before, then let this chapter begin your journey. But let me warn you now – no Hollywood horror movie could prepare you for what is going to happen when the thief arrives on earth.

Not Destined for Wrath
The Bible is clear that the judgment that is coming from the Lord is not for the believer but for the unbeliever. The Lord knows how to protect His children. One way that the Lord could spare believers is by snatching us all away in a rapture that happens before this great day of the Lord. As we study the

scriptures, we must also come to the understanding that this isn't the only way that God can protect His bride.

Psalm 91 is a great Psalm of protection that I am sure will be fulfilled over and over again during the hardships of these last days. The psalmist describes judgment happening all around him, but because he had sought shelter in the Most High God, it did not reach to him. "A thousand may fall at your side, and ten thousand at your right hand, but it shall not approach you," he wrote (Psalm 91:7). The Lordship of Jesus protects us from harm as we place our trust in Him.

Even as we look at some of the judgments of the birth pang season, we can see how the Lord is already accomplishing His protection. One great avenue of protection is obedience to His Word. I spoke before of AIDS as one of the pestilences sent by the Lord as a warning to the immoral of the world. This disease was originally transmitted by immoral behavior. People who lived under the Lordship of Christ and obeyed His commands were not targeted by this pestilence. If we obey the Lord and are virgins until our marriage, and then enjoy sex with only our marriage partner, then this disease will not target us. It did not target those who were obedient to Christ's Lordship.

I am using this example to illustrate the Lord's competence. He knows how to punish the unrighteous and save the righteous while they live together on this earth. God doesn't have to snatch us away in order to protect us. If He wishes, He can bring us through the night and preserve a remnant of us alive on the day when He returns.

There are other examples too. The two that Jesus referenced in His end time's prophecy, Noah and Lot, were also examples of how the Lord delivered the righteous and protected them under His providence, while they still lived on the earth during horrific days of judgment. God may tell us to build an ark of safety or flee from a certain area, just as He told Noah and Lot. God has His ways; we must be alert to listen to His instructions and obey His commands. No sleeping is allowed during these days.

In Revelation 7:3, before the judgment of the trumpets, God commands that His servants be marked with a mark of God on their foreheads. The judgment is not allowed to begin until these bondservants are sealed with this mark. If God knew how to number the children of Israel in the wilderness so that those over twenty received their punishment, then He knows how to protect the righteous and deliver the unrighteous to the judgment. Our job is to trust Him, listen to Him, and obey Him. That is what it means to be submitted to the Lordship of Jesus. How important it will be to have a listening ear and an obedient heart during the end times.

THE ARRIVAL OF THE THIEF

The Old Testament prophets were not the only voices warning us of the destruction of the thief. Jesus did, and so did Paul. Paul warned that sudden judgment would come like a thief in the night (I Thessalonians 5:2-3). Jesus said, "For there will be a great tribulation, such as has not occurred since the beginning of the world until now, nor ever will (Matthew 24:21)."

Do we understand that Jesus said this time would be worse than the flood that took away everyone on earth except for eight people? Very soon, the terrible day of the Lord will arrive.

THE DAY OF THE LORD
The scriptures paint a grim picture of this day. Listen to what the prophets describe:

> "Wail, for the day of the Lord is near! It will come as destruction from the Almighty. Therefore all hands will fall limp, and every man's heart will melt. They will be terrified, pains and anguish will take hold of them; they will writhe like a woman in labor, they will look at one another in astonishment, their faces aflame.
>
> Behold the day of the Lord is coming, cruel with fury and burning anger, to make the land a desolation; and He will exterminate its sinners from it. For the stars of heaven and their constellations will not flash forth their light; the sun will be dark when it rises and the moon will not shed its light. Thus I will punish the world for its evil and the wicked for their iniquity; I will also put an end to the arrogance of the proud and abase the haughtiness of the ruthless. I will make mortal man scarcer than pure gold and mankind than the gold of Ophir. Therefore I will make the heavens tremble, and the earth will be shaken from its place at the fury of the Lord of Hosts in the day of His burning anger." (Isaiah 13:6-13)
>
> "Behold, the Lord lays the earth waste, devastates it, distorts its surface and scatters its inhabitants. And the people will be like the priest, the servant like his master, the maid like her mistress, the buy-

er like the seller, the lender like the borrower, the creditor like the debtor. The earth will be completely laid waste and completely despoiled, for the Lord has spoken this word. The earth mourns and withers, the exalted of the people of the earth fade away. The earth is also polluted by its inhabitants, for they transgressed laws, violated statutes, broke the everlasting covenant. Therefore, a curse devours the earth, and those who live in it are held guilty. Therefore, the inhabitants of the earth are burned, and few men are left." (Isaiah 24:1-7)

It is hard to describe the devastation that will happen in one day. These passages I have quoted not only give us some details, but they also tell us why the judgment will come. God will abase the proud and deal with sinners who have polluted the earth with their idolatry and immorality.

It is obvious from both of these passages that the judgment on this day will be a judgment of fire; the explosions will literally cause the earth to totter and "be shaken out of its place." No matter where we live, this day will be felt throughout the whole earth.

None of us want to acknowledge that these prophecies could be describing a nuclear holocaust. I am aware that the Lord can accomplish this entirely Himself, as He has already done to Sodom and Gomorrah. However, man in his unquenchable thirst for knowledge, has discovered his own way to destroy the earth, and God is quite capable of using man's own devises to bring judgment to the earth. From Ezekiel's perspective, He does.

Gog and Magog

Ezekiel 38 and 39 describe an end time event where nations from the north try a surprise attack on Israel and are opposed by God and other nations. The result of this day is that the Lord miraculously saves Israel, and her enemies are destroyed. However, fire falls on Magog and the coastlands (Ezekiel 39:6).

In order to understand Magog, we need to take a look at the three sons of Noah and where their territories were formed. Japheth's family, Noah's oldest son, moved north into the region of Turkey and then into all of Europe. His two younger sons, Ham and Shem have been locked in a struggle for the Middle East, and in particular the land of Israel. Ham's relatives were the original settlers of Babylon and of Canaan. The people of Israel are descendents of Shem.

For many years, Bible prophets have declared that Russia is this nation of Magog who will gather other nations to come against Israel. Other Bible students think that this territory is in Turkey. Magog is a territory that is north of Israel, to be sure. Most of the nations that gather against Israel in Ezekiel 38 come from this northern region.

When speaking about the sons of Japheth in Genesis 10:5, the Bible declares that the coastlands of the nations were separated into their lands. Ezekiel claims that fire will fall on "the coastlands" during the day of the Lord. Which coastlands is Ezekiel referring to? We don't know for sure. A majority of people on earth lives on or very near the coastlands. A judgment aimed at the coastlands, as we have already witnessed during the birth pang season, can be very devastating, with great losses of life.

It is evident from this passage that God is talking about

the day of the Lord (Ezekiel 38:20, 39:8). He will prompt these northern nations to make the move on Israel that initiates this holocaust. On this day, God will be glorified, and the nations will know that God is the Holy one of Israel (Ezekiel 39:7).

THE APOSTLE JOHN'S VIEW OF THIS DAY

In the Old Testament, the trumpet was used as a call to war. The trumpet judgment found in Revelation 8 and 9 is another view of this terrible day. On the day when the first six trumpets are blown, a one third judgment encompasses the earth:

- $1/3$ of the trees are destroyed
- $1/3$ of the rivers become bitter from a star thrown to them called Wormwood
- $1/3$ of the earth is burned up
- $1/3$ of the seas become blood
- $1/3$ of the creatures in the sea will die
- $1/3$ of the ships are destroyed
- $1/3$ of the people on the earth die in this judgment

I believe John uses apocalyptic language to describe a war so devastating that it destroys one third of the entire earth. And this war doesn't last two months, two weeks, or even two days. This is the day of the Lord as the other prophets in the Bible confirm.

> "The Lord will roar from on high and utter His voice from His holy habitation; He will roar mightily against His fold. He will shout like those who tread the grapes, against all the inhabitants of the earth. A clamor has come to the end of the earth,

because the Lord has a controversy with the nations. He is entering into judgment with all flesh; as for the wicked, He has given them to the sword, declares the Lord.

Thus says the Lord of hosts, behold evil is going forth from nation to nation, and a great storm is being stirred up from the remotest parts of the earth. (In proximity to Israel, the remotest parts of the earth are where the most powerful nations live today, including Russia, China, Great Britain, and the United States.) Those slain by the Lord on that day will be from one end of the earth to the other. They will not be lamented, gathered or buried; they will be like dung on the face of the ground." (Jeremiah 25:30-33)

"Near is the great day of the Lord, near and coming very quickly; Listen, the day of the Lord! In it the warrior cries out bitterly. A day of wrath is that day, a day of trouble and distress, a day of destruction and desolation, a day of darkness and gloom, a day of clouds and thick darkness, a day of trumpet and battle cry against the fortified cities and the high corner towers. I will bring distress on men so that they will walk like the blind, because they have sinned against the Lord; and their blood will be poured out like dust and their flesh like dung. Neither their silver nor their gold will be able to deliver them on the day of the Lord's wrath; and all the earth will be devoured in the fire of His jealousy, for He will make a complete end, indeed a terrifying one of all the inhabitants of the earth." (Zephaniah 1:14-18)

Can you imagine what Zephaniah and these prophets saw? We know from Revelation that two thirds of the earth will somehow survive that day. Ezekiel and Joel both declare that Israel will be miraculously saved. But what devastation will happen on this terrible day of the Lord! If one third of humans are taken on this terrible day (Revelation 9:18), then over two billion people will die on this day! It is so horrific that we have trouble getting our minds to accept the reality of these prophecies. The world has never known a judgment like the one proclaimed in these prophecies.

The Destruction of Babylon

Revelation 17 and 18 declare that God's judgment is on Babylon, and that the mystery of Babylon will be revealed and destroyed. Her destruction will happen in one day, and her main city, which is the financial and trade center of the world, will be destroyed in one hour (Revelation 18:9).

All nations of the world comprise this Babylon. However, historically, one nation has emerged as the strongest and most powerful of its day, usually dominating the world in military might and in financial and merchant ways. This nation is always referred to as Babylon. In John's day, Rome was this nation. Many Bible scholars try to resurrect Rome or even modern-day Iraq as the end times Babylon, but they refuse to see the obvious truth.

To know the nation that epitomizes Babylon in any era of history, all you have to do is ask these simple questions and answer them honestly. Who is the most powerful military nation? Where is the biggest financial center of the world? What city, if it were destroyed in one day, would cause the entire world's economy to collapse? If you answer these questions honestly, then you know which nation and city is Babylon during your own era of history.

Revelation of Babylon

Babylon is the melting pot of religions, politics, and financial wealth. The nation and the city that takes on this identity will always have this testimony. What city and nation exemplify this beast today? Is it not New York City and the United States? Have we not been warned already?

And behold, this city is on the coastlands, exactly where the Bible states that fire will fall on the day of the Lord. To me, it is obvious that the Lord will cut off the head of Babylon on this terrible day of the Lord.

At this time, the sons of Japheth are the most powerful on the earth. If Russia, Great Britain, China, India, Pakistan, North Korea, and the United States, all of whom have nuclear capabilities, are involved in this judgment, then the balance of power in the world will shift at the end of the day. Miraculously, the Lord will save Israel, and all the rest of the surviving nations will scurry to find a leader who will oppose her.

All the attention of the earth will shift again to the Middle East. Once the sons of Japheth receive their judgment, the original conflict between Ham and Shem will remain. The middle of the earth will experience the rest of the end time troubles, as they did in early history. "And I will remove the northern army far from you, and I will drive it into a parched and desolate land. And its stench will arise and its foul smell will come up, for it has done great things (Joel 2:20)." The terrible day will destroy Japheth's dominance of power.

Babylon's Judgment

What will happen to the United States on that terrible day of the Lord? Is she not the nation who sowed the nuclear holocaust into this world? If God is not mocked, will we not reap what we have sown? Most people from the western nations are descendants of Japheth, along with Europe, and probably Asia. The United States, as well as many other nations in the remote parts of the earth, will suffer the calamity of this day.

I believe Isaiah 18 prophesies our plight on this day. Listen to its judgment – and its hope.

> "Alas, oh land of whirring wings which lies beyond the rivers of Cush, which sends envoys by the sea, even in papyrus vessels on the surface of the waters. Go swift messengers, to a nation tall and smooth, to a people feared far and wide, a powerful and oppressive nation whose land the rivers divide."

> "All you inhabitants of the world and dwellers on earth, as soon as a standard is raised on the mountains, you will see it, and as soon as the trumpet is blown, you will hear it. For thus the Lord has told me, 'I will look down from my dwelling place quietly like dazzling heat in the sunshine, like a cloud of dew in the heat of harvest.' For before the harvest, as soon as the bud blossoms and the flower becomes

a ripening grape, then He will cut off the sprigs with pruning knives and remove and cut away the spreading branches. They will be left together for birds of prey, and for the beasts of the earth; and the birds of prey will spend the summer feeding on them and the beasts of the earth will spend harvest time on them."

"At that time a gift of homage will be brought to the Lord of hosts from a people tall and smooth, even from a people feared far and wide, a powerful and oppressive nation, whose land the rivers divide – to the place of the name of the Lord of hosts, even Mount Zion."

Why do I believe that this passage is describing the United States? Let's look at the identifiers in Isaiah's prophecy. First, it is a nation of whirring wings. Isaiah couldn't say that we invented and were a land of great air travel. Those words didn't exist. His description of whirring wings was using words that were familiar to his day. Second, this nation lies beyond the rivers of Cush. Cush is often thought to be the nation we call Ethiopia. Obviously, the new world hadn't been discovered yet. But Isaiah knew that the location of this nation lay beyond Ethiopia (more west from Israel, where Isaiah gave the prophecy). It was also a land where the rivers divide. Though this might describe many nations, it certainly describes our country where the major rivers of the Mississippi, Missouri, and Ohio divide our land.

These aren't the only descriptions given. This land owns many ships, probably a great navy. They are described as a people "tall and smooth" (tall and probably clean shaven), feared far and wide, powerful and oppressive.

This nation is also capable of repenting after it is humbled, returning to its roots, and preparing an offering that is a gift of homage (allegiance) for the Lord when He returns. It is obvious that whatever remains of this nation after the terrible day of the Lord will become very aware of the kingdom of God. This same repentance occurred in our nation following the Revolutionary War and also during the Civil War.

Even the exact details of the judgment are being fulfilled as we live. The Lord states that predatory animals and birds will have a feast on the bodies of those who die in that nation on that day. This scripture couldn't have been fulfilled even thirty years ago because so many predatory animals were on the verge of extinction. This is not true today. There are so many coyotes and wolves today that some states have open hunting seasons on them. It is now possible for this scripture to be fulfilled exactly to these details.

According to Isaiah, this nation will be brought to judgment right before the harvest. The hope in this passage is that though the "branches" are cut off, survivors will remain, and they will prepare a gift of allegiance for the Lord when He comes to reign on Mount Zion.

After the day of the Lord, whatever is left of our once-proud nation will truly repent of her harlotry and return to her Christian roots, unashamedly. The survivors will spend the next seven years preparing an offering for the Lord, a gift they will give Him to show their allegiance to Him. Hopefully included in this offering will be the repentant souls that will be saved for His kingdom following this terrible day.

THE MOST PROPHESIED DAY OF THE BIBLE

This terrible day of the Lord is prophesied over and over again in the Bible. It will bring mighty nations to their knees in a single day. Since the population of the earth is so much greater today, the judgment of this day will be unparalleled. More people will die on this day than on any other day in history. This day begins a season of judgment, as God contends with the nations who have not received His glorious reign.

In other generations, it would have been impossible for a third of the earth to be destroyed in one day, at least by man's devices, but not in ours. We all know it is possible. It is the most sobering thought.

For so long, we haven't entertained the idea of such destruction because we believe that no one will put a finger on the button to start this chaos. Yet nations have not stopped devising more ways to gain power and destroy to a greater capacity. There is absolutely no historical evidence of nations creating weapons and not using them. We live in a sad day, and we deceive only ourselves by believing that the world will never be forced into using these weapons.

According to Ezekiel 38, God Himself will bring the nations to this brink. He will put hooks into the jaws of the northern nations and bring them down against Israel, to reveal His great power and glory. This day is His day.

MIRACULOUS SAVING POWER

The real miracle is that, somehow, two-thirds of the earth will survive this day. With the capabilities of these nations to destroy, only the intervention of the Lord will save the earth from total destruction.

The focus of the scriptures is Israel's salvation on that day. Only a direct intervention of the Lord will save Israel from experiencing the consequences of this day. I believe that not only will God intervene in Israel, He will completely direct and intervene all over the world that day.

Ezekiel 39:6 – "And I shall send fire upon Magog and those who inhabit the coastlands in safety; and they will know that I am the Lord."

Fire will fall in the coastland regions of the world and upon Magog who is the initiator of this battle. Possibly, many other "would be hits" will be diverted into the oceans and seas, as God protects some places from imminent disaster. The Word is clear that even one third of the waters of the earth will be affected by this judgment, and that is a lot of territory. Again, this alone could create utter havoc along the coastlands, where the majority of people live.

That doesn't necessarily mean that the inland or mountain regions will be completely safe. There are many scriptures that speak of men crawling into caves and asking the mountains to fall on them and hide them from the disaster of this day. The only safe place on earth that day is to be in Christ, listening to His direct orders and obeying what He tells us to do. He will protect His bride from disaster.

I know that this day belongs to the Lord, that He will direct the judgment and save His people. It will be a day of His divine intervention into the affairs of man, both to bring judgment and to save. This day is His day. He is the judge; He will decide.

Our generation of preachers has been blind to this day. The preaching of this generation has emphasized God's love over His judgment. For many believers, the idea of judgment is a foreign concept. We have almost single-handedly rocked the church to sleep, into thinking that they won't be here when the tough times come. Yet, it is in the New Testament that the writer of Hebrews warns us, "It is a terrifying thing to fall into the hands of the living God." We cannot keep living immoral and idolatrous lifestyles and not expect judgment.

The Feast of the Trumpets will announce the day of the Lord and begin the 70th week of Daniel. This day is like no other in history, and it will come like a thief in the night. God will begin, control, judge, save, and end this terrible day. All the nations involved are just players; the story of this day has already been written. The truth is this day will have an affect on all nations, regardless who is spared and who is destroyed. It will cause all of the survivors to tremble and wonder – if that was the first day, what will happen next? There are seven more years of judgment and turmoil.

Chapter Five
DAY TWO—
THE RISE OF ANTICHRIST

II Thessalonians 2:3 - "Let no one in any way deceive you, for it will not come unless the apostasy comes first, and the man of lawlessness is revealed, the son of destruction."

It is hard to imagine what Day Two will look like after the terrible day of the Lord. The earth will be devastated and according to the Word, actually be shaken out of its place. How will that affect the weather and seasons afterwards? How long will it take the survivors to realize that their lives will not return to what they once knew? The Bible gives us some details of the immediate season that follows the terrible day of the Lord. I have labeled this season, Day Two.

Certainly, Israel will rejoice and develop a new recognition of the God who saved her. However, she won't bow her knee to the Lord Jesus Christ yet. I believe there will be a new freedom in Israel to accomplish things that her people feared to do under Babylon's great pressure. Now that Babylon's power is weakened, she will build the temple she has long desired.

"Thus says the Lord God, 'When I gather the house of Israel from the peoples among whom they are

> scattered, and will manifest My holiness in them in the sight of the nations, then they will live in the land which I gave to my servant Jacob. They will live in it securely; and they will build houses, plant vineyards, and live securely when I execute judgments upon all who scorn them round about them. Then they will know that I am the Lord their God." (Ezekiel 28:25-26)

Day Two will be a day of revelation of the God of Israel, but not in a New Testament sense. Israel will no longer be a secular nation like she is today but will receive a revelation of God's intervention. She will return to a new understanding of her Old Testament roots. Sacrificial worship will be reinstated in Israel again.

I believe another temple patterned either after Solomon's or Herod's temple will be built during the early part of the tribulation, if not started before it. For a short season, Israel will have great boldness to return to her Old Testament foundations by building this temple. Needless to say, this will incense other nations.

Unfortunately, the terrible treatment of the Palestinians may worsen once this Babylonian pressure is relieved. If Israel treats them harshly now, while the world watches, what will she do when she has no one to answer to? Remember, Israel hasn't bowed her knee to Jesus yet. Loving her enemy has never been a part of her doctrine.

The rest of the world won't need an excuse to band together against Israel, for they have always hated this nation and have historically treated her with contempt. The polarization of these nations will certainly not be new.

There are several passages of scripture that proclaim Israel's deliverance from the terrible atrocities of the day of the Lord. The whole story of Israel's gathering together and her deliverance can be found in Ezekiel 36-39. Ezekiel warns Israel that her gathering and deliverance is a result of the Lord's plan and mercy, but not Israel's righteousness. Joel also prophesies the deliverance of Israel from the day of the Lord (Joel 2:18-20).

While Israel is strengthening her Old Testament roots, a new ruler will emerge of many of her surrounding nations. There appears to be a season of tranquility. After the destruction of the day of the Lord, the world will welcome this rest and begin a journey to security again. However, there will be no peace.

Many books have already been written trying to depict what will happen next. Most have been written from the perspective that the church was removed from the earth. I don't want to speculate about this time period. I am only interested in Bible study and what the Bible has to say. Let's try to put together some of the scriptures about this season, without getting dogmatic about timelines.

THE APOSTASY AND THE RISE OF THE ANTICHRIST

Antichrist spirits have been among us for a long time and have always tried to destroy the people of God and God's coming kingdom. The antichrist is the false messiah, one who will try to gather and then control the whole world system in one last stand of Babylon the Great (Revelation 13 and Daniel 11). Roman emperors attempted this total dominance. So did Hitler, Haman, Nebuchadnezzar, and a host of others too numerous to mention. Every one of them targeted the people of God and tried to exterminate them. They all have received – and will receive – the same fate. The Lord has always intervened and destroyed them.

There is a real correlation in Scripture between apostasy, the falling away from the faith, and the antichrist spirit (II Thessalonians 2:3 and Daniel 7:25). When this spirit is strong, it wears down the saints. It is important during this current season that we correctly identify this spirit, as it is already at work in the world (I John 4:3). The person of the antichrist doesn't just appear; he will be groomed and empowered by a spirit already at work.

This "wearing down of the saints" is the falling away from the faith that much of the church is experiencing, giving in to the world's agenda and pressure, rather than holding fast to the Word of God. The church is not the only institution succumbing to this pressure. Businesses, cities, nations, sports teams, and all facets of society are making decisions today that align with this spirit's agenda. Standards of morality that have been the moor of society for thousands of years are being abandoned and condemned. The antichrist spirit's influence is taking over the world.

THE APOSTASY IN THE WORLD AND THE CHURCH

Paul warned Timothy of this falling away and even prophetically described the day that now has come upon us. I Timothy 4:1-3 says, "But the Spirit explicitly says that in later times some will fall away from the faith, paying attention to deceitful spirits and doctrines of demons, by means of the hypocrisy of liars seared in their own conscience as with a branding iron, men who forbid marriage and advocate abstaining from foods which God has created to be gratefully shared in by those who believe and know the truth."

I remember reading this passage years ago, skeptical that marriage and food would become the issues of apostasy. Twenty years ago, this passage of scripture seemed too distant and improbable to be fulfilled. But as always, prophecy is much better at seeing the future than I will ever be. These words have already been fulfilled, literally.

Who would believe that a man's business could be targeted and hated because he stated strongly his belief in marriage? Who would believe the onslaught of young adults who live together and never even consider God's plan in marriage? Who would believe that the church of the living God would begin to marry same-sex couples, defend their rights, and refuse to confront their own people who live together in unrighteousness, outside the confines of Biblical marriage? Paul saw clearly the issue of the apostasy.

Our society is also obsessed with healthy living. Healthy living is the new fountain of youth that every one is searching for, hoping to find the right pill or food to eradicate our diseases and keep us young. Our society is flooded with health remedies of every kind, and advice on what foods to eat and what not to eat. Our new god is to live as long as we can by eating right or taking the right pill. We are absolutely infatuated with the idea of extending our lives here, while all the time, judgment day is looming.

If only we were that concerned with our spiritual health. Paul states in this same passage, "for bodily discipline is only of little profit, but godliness is profitable for all things, since it holds promise for the present life and also for the life to come (I Timothy 4:6)."

The apostasy is in our midst, and the falling away from the faith has already begun. The issues are exactly the ones that Paul predicted they would be. The spirit of antichrist is wearing down both the church and our society, causing us to rewrite history and change the oldest, most established boundaries of mankind. The spirit of antichrist wants us to bow our knees to his agenda and forsake the Lordship of Jesus Christ.

Antichrist Spirit Precedes the Man of Lawlessness

If this spirit exerts this kind of pressure now and has already caused the church to wear down and accept his agenda, what will happen when a ruling king personifies this spirit? We have witnessed this spirit's onslaught in Germany, Russia, and China, and we have seen how it controls through fear. This spirit will dictate what you are allowed to buy and sell, where you can live, who you may worship, and will despise certain ethnic backgrounds. The world has promised "never again" to allow this spirit to oppress – yet it operates from this spirit in everything that it does.

It does not matter who the person of antichrist is, where he comes from, or when he will arrive. While we are looking for a person, this spirit is already menacing the land. **HE IS ALREADY AT WORK!** I care about the thousands of people who say they are believers, but who don't live within the boundaries of the Lordship of Jesus. They are deceived and have moved themselves into the line of fire, becoming a target for the thief.

We are at this hour because we deserve to be here. God has

given us over to the immoral lifestyle that we have championed for so many years (Romans 1:24). It should not surprise us that the world is exerting this pressure, but it is so disheartening to see much of the church, which bears the name of the Lord, giving in to this agenda. This church is largely self-ruled, with hirelings as leaders. They are weary of proclaiming righteousness, even in the church, where parents often defend their children's immoral behavior or practice the same.

What will become of the church that defends same-sex marriage and gives in to the pressure of the world in lowering moral standards? What will become of the church that defends a woman's right to choose and stands in agreement with the killing of millions of innocent unborn children? We are still guilty of bowing our knees to Molech and worshipping the immoral Ashtoreth by the decisions that we make. These Old Testament gods commanded child sacrifice and sexual immorality as rites of worship. May God have mercy on our souls, and may we wake up and repent before it is too late.

Paul told the Thessalonian church that our gathering together unto Him at the Lord's return would not happen until the apostasy takes place and the man of lawlessness is revealed (II Thessalonians 2:1-3). Paul said this man would exalt himself above every so-called god and object of worship, so that he takes his seat in the temple of God, displaying himself as God. He also proclaimed that the mystery of lawlessness is already at work.

Daniel saw him coming, too. In Daniel 7:24-25, this king rises and subdues three other nations or kings while he is gaining great power. He will speak out against the Most High God and wear down the saints. He will also make alterations in times and laws. Later, in the eleventh chapter, Daniel says this one will have no desire for women or any regard for the gods of his fathers, but will instead honor a god of fortresses. We see this spirit already at work, paving the way for the man to follow.

As the remaining nations of this world gather in fear and hatred of Israel, the last seven years of this age will focus again on the Middle East, just as the early years of earth's history did. The powerful nations in the most remote parts of the earth have now been humbled by the day of the Lord. The antichrist will be granted power by many nations, who join their forces together against Israel. Although they will declare a new season of peace for the earth, there will be no peace.

THE CONTINUED JUDGMENTS

During this time, the earth will continue to suffer under the effects of the relentless judgment. A large portion of the earth has been so destroyed that nothing is able to live there. In these places, the dead are not buried but lie on the ground and provide food for the beasts of the earth and the birds of the sky. John tells us in Revelation 8 that many men die because they drink the "bitter" water of Wormwood. This reference could easily describe water that is tainted with radiation poisoning. The judgment that began on the day of the Lord will continue its onslaught.

What will Day Two be like? The Bible warns us of this time

SEVEN MONTHS OF BURYING THE DEAD IN ISRAEL

The armies of the nations that gathered against Israel will die on the northern mountain regions of Israel. God will miraculously save Israel, and there will be so much confusion that the armies will turn on and destroy one other. One can only imagine our reactions to the earth shaking and tottering out of its place. The Lord will roar on the day of the Lord, and those coming against Israel will be destroyed.

Ezekiel states that it will take Israel seven months to bury the dead and remove the uncleanness from the land. Seven months later, they will still be finding skeleton remains of the armies that came against her on the day of the Lord. Also, they will burn the weapons of warfare for the next seven years. They won't have to gather wood for fuel to keep warm during the winters because they will burn the weapons that these nations brought against them.

City of Chaos

The Lord showed Isaiah some of the difficulties the survivors will have in the nations who are judged on the day of the Lord. Zephaniah saw areas of complete destruction, but Isaiah saw the survivors that lived and told us plainly of the difficulties they will face in Day Two.

Isaiah 24:10 says, "The city of chaos is broken down; every house is shut up so that none may enter." It doesn't take much imagination to picture what will happen after this day. New Orleans and Los Angeles have already experienced how quickly an ordered society can break down into cities of chaos. All over the world, looting and chaos will abound in nations that no longer have the ability to police themselves. People will be frightened and worried about how they will survive. They will loot stores in search of food and security. The problem is, stores can only be looted one time. Then, people will begin to turn on each other and break into each other's homes. It will not be a pleasant time to live, especially in cities.

Financial Collapse

According to Revelation 18, the most important financial city of the world will be destroyed in one hour. The merchants of the earth all weep and cry, wondering how they will sell and market their goods. Isaiah 24:2 states that the people will become like the priest, the servant like his master, the maid like her mistress, the buyer like the seller, the lender like the borrower, the creditor like the borrower. After the holocaust, it won't matter what you did before the Day. All lives will change, and everyone will be in the same boat together.

Ezekiel 7:19 states that we will throw our silver and gold into the streets, for it cannot satisfy our appetites. Food and shelter from the heat and the cold will be the only things that matter to the survivors of the day of the Lord. Our idols, everything that we relied on in the past, will be destroyed and taken from us.

Great Mourning

Can you imagine a holocaust event coming upon our society with no warning? How many people will be separated from their families on this day? If communications are wiped out on that day – and they probably will be – how will we know the condition of our loved ones who live in another part of the country or who were traveling away from home on that day?

"Even when their survivors escape, they will be on the mountains like doves of the valleys, all of them mourning, each over his own iniquity. All hands will hang limp, and all knees will become like water (Ezekiel 7:16-17)."

The Bible is clear there will be great mourning on Day Two as families try to find their loved ones, hear of who survived, and try to find out which areas were totally destroyed. Ezekiel and Isaiah proclaim the mourning that will cover the earth on Day Two. Nothing that mankind has ever gone through will compare with that day.

People Fleeing, Trying to Return Home

Isaiah sees the turmoil of this day and writes, "And it will be like a hunted gazelle, or like sheep with none to gather them, they will each turn to his own people and each one flee to his own land (Isaiah 13:14)." Amos and the other prophets warn of the confusion and fleeing that will happen after this day. "There is wailing in all the plazas, and in all the streets they say 'Alas! Alas!' For what purpose will the day of the Lord be to you? It will be darkness and not light; as when a man flees from a lion and a bear greets him, or goes home, leans his hand against the wall and a snake bites him. Will not the day of the Lord be darkness instead of light, even gloom with no brightness in it (Amos 5:16,18-20)?"

This day will be just like September 11, 2001, only a million times worse. I lived in Somerset County, Pennsylvania, just fifteen miles from where Flight 93 went down. After the plane crashed near Shanksville, people left their jobs in droves. The only thing that local parents could think about was retrieving their school children and bringing them home. We had no idea why our rural county had been targeted along with New York City and Washington D.C. that day. This day was a small harbinger of what is to come.

All over the world, families will try to reunite and attempt to get back to their homes. Mourning will fill our streets and hysteria our land. We will not know about the condition of our loved ones living or visiting in other parts of the world.

Hands Hanging Limp, Hearts that Melt, and Faces Aflame

Isaiah describes the condition of the survivors in Isaiah 13:7-8. Everyone's hands will hang limp and all the strength in their bodies will drain out of them. Not only have millions upon millions just died in one day, the survivors are a people accustomed to a life of relative ease. How will that pampered generation survive the next seven years until Jesus returns?

There may also be the effects of radiation poisoning that many will have to go through after this judgment (their faces aflame Isaiah 13:8). Even though one-third of the earth was already destroyed in one day, the effects of that day will continue to claim more and more lives. Ezekiel says that famine and plague will overcome those in cities (Ezekiel 7:15). With so much death surrounding them and no hospital care available, more and more will die during the following days, weeks, and months. They will lose their hope, unless the bride of Christ rescues them.

Death will surround the living. Dead fish and other aquatic life will wash up on the beaches. Human remains will be so numerous that they will not be buried but left for vultures and other animals to eat. As it was in former times, disease and pestilence will follow on the heels of decaying bodies.

Night Will Come

If the Lord wishes to take away all of our idols, then all He has to do is unplug us. If, indeed, it is a nuclear holocaust that is portrayed by these prophets, then it is probable that most, if not the entire electric grid of the earth, will be destroyed in that one day. Since nations have no way of defending themselves against a nuclear attack, exploding bombs above their enemies will send an electromagnetic pulse that can take out the power, destroying their capability to strike back. Almost any nuclear warhead that day will have the capability to explode above the atmosphere and cause a shock wave that will disable electronics. Without electricity, water cannot be pumped, hospitals and modern medicine will lose the ability to function, and every aspect of modern life will cease. Everything in our current lifestyle is dependent on electricity. It will become night on earth.

I know that I am painting a very grim picture of what awaits the nations on the day of the Lord. Those who are lofty will be brought down. The Bible gives us great detail of what will happen on Day Two. We must be prepared for the inevitable coming of this day.

The Humble will be Left

The Bible also states that God will destroy the arrogant and the arrogance of the earth on that day (Isaiah 13:11). Zephaniah 3:12 says, "But I will leave among you a humble and lowly people and they will take refuge in the name of the Lord." Isaiah 24:9 says, "All night long my soul longs for You, indeed, my spirit within me seeks You diligently; for when the earth experiences Your judgments the inhabitants of the world learn righteousness."

Humility leads men back to Jesus. Humility is always the door to the kingdom of God. Though no one wishes to live through a tragedy of this magnitude, one of the results will be that men's hearts will be open to the gospel of Jesus. Mankind always learns righteousness after the judgment.

THE BRIDE WILL ARISE!

It is sobering to realize what must happen to humble mankind and bring him back to his King and his Savior. Many will be bitter and become even more hardened by the judgment, as Pharaoh did. But the Bible declares with great boldness that the people who know their God will do mighty exploits and lead many to righteousness. (Daniel 11:32,33 and 12:3)

I believe that the great harvest of righteousness will take place during the early part of the tribulation, following the great judgment of the day of the Lord. If people don't come to know Jesus after this event, then they will likely continue to harden their hearts to destruction. Christ's bride, prepared and ready, will gather the lost souls after this great judgment day.

The longer the judgments are poured out, the less people repent and the more they are hardened for the final judgment. The latter part of the tribulation will probably see little reaping of souls. Just as God closed the door of the ark to Noah's generation, and hardened the hearts of the Israelites during Paul's generation, so it appears that God will call the Gentiles to salvation one last time. In Revelation 9:20 and 16:11, people became more hardened by the difficulties of the tribulation. They will be under the heavy influence of the antichrist spirit as he bears down on the world. Night will come, and no man will work (John 9:4).

What will happen to us if we are unprepared for this time? I shudder to think of the judgment on the unprepared church. So many are sleeping and have no awareness at all of the day of the Lord. Many others live in fear of this day and want to store large supplies of food and have weapons ready to defend their stash. Why would we act so selfishly during the days when the Lord expects a great harvest?

Others don't even want to bring themselves to think about this time and simply ignore every warning sign. Who will be the wise virgins of our day and prepare for this day with the oil of the Lord? Who will be the people who know their God, who display strength, take action, and lead many to righteousness?

Though no one wishes for the death of more than two billion people in one day (a third of the earth's population), yet this day will come, and nothing will stop its arrival. The Bible states it will be released on the exact day and hour that God has prepared it for (Revelation 9:15). Psalm 91 will be fulfilled on this day as God protects His church on earth by hiding her in His shadow and then releases her for this major season of harvest.

Workmen who are not Ashamed

It is time to study the Word and prepare for the day of the Lord. This day will be a time of great hardship, yet a remnant will escape and remain for the coming of the Lord. Amidst the horrors of that day, Isaiah hears worship coming from the west, and the east, and even from the severely judged coastlands (Isaiah 24:14-15). A great revival will occur during the early season of the tribulation. A people will be made ready like a bride for the coming of the Lord. They will come out of the tribulation with white robes of righteousness.

Pastors, have you prepared your people for the coming of this day? Do you understand what is shortly coming to this earth? Is your ear attentive and your heart soft to do exactly as the Lord directs you as this day approaches? "But you brethren are not in darkness that the day would overtake you like a thief (I Thessalonians 5:4)."

Believers, even if your pastor hasn't prepared you, you have the Word, and it is readily available to you. As the prophet Amos so boldly proclaimed, "Prepare to meet your God, O Israel!"

So many in the body of Christ are unprepared students of the end times, though many have watched movies about it. Many teachers have declared the rapture to be the feast of Trumpets, rather than the day of the Lord, when the six trumpet judgment will come upon the earth. This little twist of focus has put us to sleep. We must awaken to all that the Bible declares will happen in the end times.

> "Be on guard, that your hearts may not be weighted down with dissipation and drunkenness and the worries of life, and that day come on you suddenly like a trap; for it will come upon all those who dwell on the face of the earth. But keep alert at all times, praying in order that you may have strength to escape all these things that are about to take place, and to stand before the Son of Man." (Luke 21:34-36)

Some believers joke about the end times declaring that they are "pan" millennialists because they believe that everything will "pan" out in the end. We sadly joke as if these times will not be difficult, as though it is impossible to understand what the prophets are saying.

It does take careful listening, the revelation of the Holy Spirit, to understand the day of the Lord. We only have a brief moment left to study and prepare ourselves for the inevitable coming of the day of the Lord.

Day Two, the early days of the tribulation, will come. Israel will return to her roots; antichrist will arise, and amidst the horror of the tribulation of those days and the chaos that results, a people who know their God will perform mighty exploits and lead many to righteousness.

How are they able to do these exploits? They are able to do them because they are prepared for this day and have sought the Lord for His strength and anointing to lead many to righteousness. They are not surprised by the day of the Lord or about how difficult it will be following this day. This bride will not be selfish people, concerned only about their own welfare. They will understand the hour and give of themselves to bless others.

Every human fulfills the prophecy of the Bible. Some are part of the great apostasy, some sleep, and some prepare. Others are uncaring, immoral, and will become the target of the judgments that are being poured out. The love of some will grow cold, while others keep the flame burning and prepare for the great day. Which prophesy do you fulfill?

> "Multitudes, multitudes in the valley of decision! For the day of the Lord is near in the valley of decision." (Joel 3:14)

Chapter Six
THE TIME OF JACOB'S TROUBLE

Jeremiah 30:7 – "Alas for that day is great, there is none like it; and it is the time of Jacob's distress, but he will be saved from it."

Ezekiel 20:35-38 – "And I will bring you into the wilderness of the peoples, and there I will enter into judgment with you face to face. As I entered into judgment with your fathers in the wilderness or the land of Egypt, so I will enter into judgment with you," declares the Lord God. "I will make you pass under the rod, and I will bring you into the bond of the covenant; and I will purge from you the rebels and those who transgress against Me; I will bring them out of the land where they sojourn, but they will not enter into the land of Israel. Thus you will know that I am the Lord."

Israel's revival will be short, and her time of rejoicing will not last long as the nations surrounding her will begin to gather together. Though they speak peace for a season, this peace will not last long. The spirit of antichrist is deceptive and will always try to wear down and then destroy the people of God. This is and always has been its nature.

I believe in the person of the antichrist. All throughout history, one individual person has risen as Satan's pawn, attempting to destroy the plans, purpose, and people of God. Hitler was the last really strong one; but many since him have spewed their hatred and their bitterness at the people of God. The ruler of Iran has such a spirit, though he has never gained much power outside his own country. He remains a constant threat to Israel.

According to Daniel, the antichrist ruler will not promote the religion of his fathers. Whether he comes from Christian, Moslem, or some other background, he will rise to power on the wings of compromise. Compromise has always been Satan's secret weapon of rebellion, for it removes the Lordship of Christ. This spirit of compromise has already captured and enslaved many in the church and has already caused the apostasy of the end times.

Zechariah, Daniel, Ezekiel, and the Apostle John were all given revelation of this last season of this age. Jeremiah also saw this day and called this time, "the time of Jacob's trouble." In this passage of Jeremiah 30, God promises to "destroy completely" all nations where Israel had previously been scattered. He will also chasten Israel and will not leave them unpunished (verse 11). The last years of this age will be another time of great trouble to Israel and continued judgments on the nations.

As Apostle John declares in Revelation 13, the person of antichrist will rule in the surrounding nations of Israel and influence the entire world. Almost all nations will hear of him and begin to worship and submit to him. Yet according to Daniel, he will have trouble spots and other kings rising up to oppose him. And of course, Israel will find herself in the center of these conflicts.

Israel will also discover that she is alone during this season.

She can no longer rely on the help that the United States and Great Britain had provided before the day. Though Israel will rejoice over her deliverance, the sudden reality of her precarious position will soon sink in. Her people are all alone now. They must return to trust in their God and in His ability to protect them.

Daniel does not portray the antichrist ruling the entire world, but he does gain strength and become a king and military ruler of many nations. In Daniel, there is a king of the South (perhaps nations from Africa who survived the day) who fights against this king of the North. The antichrist will discover, just as Hitler did, that not everybody will worship and bow to his image, though he remains convinced that some day they all will. He will attempt to overtake and rule the world, as Hitler and every other antichrist has done before him.

This antichrist kingdom will be established with the help of religious leaders. In particular, one major leader will give his power and allegiance to this beast (Revelation 13 and 17). The story of Babylon plays itself out again, even after the judgment of the day of the Lord. This mixing of religion and politics has defined Babylon's history. There really is nothing new under the sun.

The antichrist will bring out an old form of self-worship; one that Nebuchadnezzar implemented six hundred years before Christ came. Antichrist is always about proclaiming oneself to be God, and this exactly what the antichrist will do again. You would think that after the day of the Lord, man might have learned his lesson, yet he continues to build another kingdom that is not submitted to the Lordship of Jesus. This is the way of Babylon the Great.

The antichrist will be charismatic, deceptive, and brilliant, but also arrogant, which will lead to his downfall. In the midst of the greatest world crisis that man has ever faced, he will gather nations and gain strength. He will put together a new financial system that will only allow a man to buy and sell if he has the mark, the infamous mark of the beast. The antichrist will cause men in his nations to forsake their former religions by demonstrating demonic power that will deceive many. Then, he will command that they all worship him and his image. Some major religious leader will confirm his lordship and herald him as the world's messiah. All of this is recorded in Revelation 13.

Meanwhile, a conglomerate of nations ruled by this powerful beast now surrounds Israel. Apparently, this ruler has the freedom to go in and out of Israel on his way to conquer the nations of the south. It won't take long to weaken the power of Israel who will be alienated and cut off from the other nations. Daniel 11:28-45 tells the story of this ruler and gives us the details of his plundering of Jerusalem and of Israel. Zechariah also declares that many in Jerusalem will be taken captive again and be exiled, and Ezekiel confirms this. This antichrist king appears too strong for the nation of Israel, and at least four different times he will pass through her land.

The first time, in Daniel 11:28, he takes action and then returns to his own land. What action does he take? We don't know. He probably threatens them and begins to wear them down, as Daniel saw earlier in chapter seven. Later, he will go against the southern nations, but this time they offer great opposition, which actually disheartens the antichrist. At this point, he turns and takes his frustrations out on Israel.

Daniel says this ruler (Daniel never uses the term, antichrist) will show regard for those who forsake the holy covenant. Apparently, Israel will have many defectors willing to give their allegiance to this king, probably because of the economic pressures they are under. His forces will enter into the sanctuary fortress and desecrate it, stopping the daily sacrifices. This antichrist ruler seems too strong for Israel to defeat.

The apostle Paul declares (along with Daniel) that the antichrist will take his seat in the temple of God and declare himself to be God. Daniel says he will speak monstrous things against the God of gods. For a season, he will prosper and afflict the nation of Israel. They are troubled again and being tested to see if they will trust in their God. Israel and many others will have to choose whether they will give in to this economic pressure and take the mark of the beast. They will be tested and tempted to compromise their standards in order to survive.

There will be faithful Israelis and probably strong Christians living in Israel who will not give in to this pressure and who will lead many away from the influence of this antichrist. But many of them will fall and be martyred. Some will escape. Two witnesses (seen both by Zechariah and by John, in Revelation 11) will begin to prophesy in Jerusalem and declare the purposes of God with signs and wonders. They will prophesy for a period of time in what appears to be the last half of the tribulation. The surrounding nations, and even Israel, will be troubled by the appearance of these two witnesses.

When this season reaches its climactic end, the antichrist will once again march through Israel in order to face the southern opposition. This time he will have great success in Egypt and in northern Africa. On his way back to the north, this arrogant conqueror will stop in Israel and set up his tents in the valley of Megiddo. Possibly, at this time, he will enter Jerusalem, kill the two witnesses, and make strong threats against Israel and the city of Jerusalem. He has determined to destroy them.

A season that began with great joy in Israel, as they were delivered from the terrible day of the Lord's judgment, will end with the threat of annihilation again. The surrounding nations sit on Jerusalem's doorstep in the valley of Megiddo. Israel has no more hope. Their history has caught up with them once more. Another Nebuchadnezzar has surrounded them, and there is no other nation left in this world willing to help or intervene.

The last days of the tribulation are a tremendous testing time for Israel and for the believers who remain. Malachi speaks of these days and says, "So you will again distinguish between the righteous and wicked, between the one who serves God and one who does not serve Him (Malachi 3:18)." Israel will be divided again; many will compromise and become traitors as they give in to this pressure of the antichrist. Taking the mark will be the physical sign of inner depravity, compromise, apostasy, and the certain judgment that is to come.

The time of Jacob's trouble are the dark days of confrontation between Israel and the antichrist. The purpose is to winnow, purge, and purify those who remain. Jerusalem, in particular, will suffer during these days. The antichrist will plan for the total destruction of that city and, ultimately, the entire nation of Israel.

As these armies gather in the valley of Megiddo, the hope of Israel is almost extinguished. Will she be destroyed again? Will history repeat itself? Will God give His people over to these nations to be destroyed and scattered again?

There is no human agency of hope left. If ever Israel needed her Messiah, it will be on this day. Another significant day of the Lord has come. Though the antichrist has continually grown stronger and more confident, his pride will lead him to a tremendous fall. God will not abandon His people. For there is yet another day to come in the glorious day of the Lord and another great feast to be fulfilled.

THE DAY

PART 3:

THE DAY OF THE LORD—
THE DAY OF HIS RETURN

Chapter Seven

THE MARRIAGE SUPPER OF THE LAMB

Revelation 19:9 – "Blessed are those who are invited to the marriage supper of the Lamb."

Revelation 19:17 – "Come assemble for the great supper of God, so that you may eat the flesh of kings and the flesh of commanders and the flesh of mighty men and the flesh of horses and of those who sit on them and the flesh of all men, both free men and slaves, and small and great."

Many times in Israel's history enemies have surrounded her. As a result of these judgment times, many Israelites lost their lives; some were taken captive and then scattered throughout the earth. Assyria conquered the Northern Kingdom of Israel in 722 B.C. Babylon destroyed the Southern Kingdom of Judah and Jerusalem in 586 B.C. Rome did the same thing in A.D. 70, and the city of Jerusalem was trampled underfoot by Gentiles from that day until 1967. Charged with being a light to the world and a people for God's own possession, the people of Israel have often found themselves carrying a heavy burden. Israel has struggled with her calling, suffering the consequences of apostasy many times.

And once again, Israel is surrounded by all the nations submitted to the antichrist. They are spread out over the valley of Armageddon waiting to devour her. She doesn't have a chance in this world of surviving; but her help is not of this world.

Israel's salvation from the terrible day of the Lord had nothing to do with her repentance, righteousness, or any good works that she had done. It was only the Lord's mercy that accomplished her deliverance. Despite her shortcomings, her sin, rebellion, and rejection of the Messiah when He first came to her, God still loves Israel, saving her for His purposes in the last days.

Although the stage is set for another annihilation of Israel, the end of this age is at hand. Jesus, the Lord, is coming to intervene, and a new story is about to be introduced to the world. But He doesn't come alone.

Gathering of the Saints

The English word "rapture" is not found in the Bible. The continual theme of this event in the Bible is the gathering together of the saints to the Lord. The following passages of scripture confirm this:

> "But immediately **after** the tribulation of those days the sun will be darkened, and the moon will not give its light, and the stars will fall from the sky, and the powers of the heavens will be shaken. And then the sign of the Son of Man will appear in the sky, and then all the tribes of the earth will mourn, and they will see the Son of Man coming on the clouds of the sky with power and great glory. And He will send forth His angels with a great trumpet

and they will **gather** together His elect from the four winds, from one end of the sky to the other." (Matthew 24:29-31)

"Now we request you, brethren, with regard to the coming of our Lord Jesus Christ and our **gathering together** to Him." (II Thessalonians 2:1)

"For the Lord Himself will descend from heaven with a shout, with the voice of the archangel and with the trumpet of God, and the dead in Christ will rise first. Then, we who are alive and remain will **be caught up together with them** in the clouds to meet the Lord in the air, and so we shall always be with the Lord." (I Thessalonians 4:16-17)

"And then He will send forth the angels, and will **gather together His elect** from the four winds, from the farthest end of the earth to the farthest end of heaven." (Mark 13:27)

At the end of this age, the final victory is not just for Jesus; it is also for all of the righteous men and women of God who trusted in Jesus during this age. This victory began between the death and resurrection of Jesus during the early season of the day of the Lord. Ephesians 4:8-10 tells us that when Jesus died, He descended into Hades where the Old Testament saints were waiting in a place called Abraham's bosom (Luke 16:22). The first sign of Jesus' reign occurred after He died. He spoke to the gates of this place, which burst open, and these saints were free to ascend to heaven to be with the Lord. The Old Testament saints were rescued from Hades and have spent the last two thousand years in the presence of the Lord in heaven. They experienced the first victory of the kingdom of Jesus.

The second aspect of this victory is found in both I Thessalonians 4:13 and Philippians 1:23. After the resurrection of Jesus, what fate awaited the death of the righteous? The early church asked this question while they were waiting for the return of Jesus. Since there was a delay in His return, some of the brethren were dying. What became of them? Were they just sleeping until the resurrection of the dead?

Paul answers this question in these two different passages. He assures the believers in both passages that the dead in Christ go to be with the Lord immediately upon their death. Because of Christ's resurrection, they are granted the privilege of being united with Christ in their death, then returning with Jesus when He comes back.

These departed saints of God have not yet experienced the resurrection of their new bodies as they wait in heaven for us to fulfill our mission. Hebrews 12 gives us a picture of them gathered together, cheering us on as we faithfully continue the struggle of righteousness on earth. Even in heaven, the martyred souls of the departed are crying out to the Lord, "How long, O Lord, holy and true, will You refrain from judging and avenging our blood on those who dwell on the earth (Revelation 6:10)?" They are restless, anxious to see the fulfillment of the kingdom of God.

THE LAST TRUMPET

Earlier, on the terrible day of the Lord, six trumpets were blown and one-third of the earth was destroyed. As I mentioned, trumpets were used to gather people, usually for war. When Jesus comes, every passage about His return includes a trumpet blast. This will be the last time that a trumpet sounds to gather people for a war. Wars are about to end forever.

THE ANNOUNCEMENT

Revelation 11:15 - And the seventh angel sounded and there arose loud voices in heaven saying, "**The kingdom of the world has become the kingdom of our Lord, and of His Christ; and He will reign forever and ever.**" Yes, the Lord is returning at the sound of the trumpet, but He also has a Christ. The anointed ones, those who believed and lived under His Lordship, are about to be gathered for the last battle of mankind.

The purpose of the gathering together of the saints is first and foremost, to receive the reward of our new, resurrected bodies. Those who have already died return with the Lord in soul and spirit; they will be the first to come to the earth and rise out of the ground to receive their new resurrected bodies, which I Corinthians 15 tells us are imperishable. Sorry Batman, Spiderman, and Superman – the real thing is far better than make believe.

The believers still alive on earth at the coming of the Lord will also be transformed and changed in a twinkling of an eye. They, too, will rise to meet the Lord in the air. For the first time in history, all saints in God are together with Christ. Instead of going to heaven, as we have been led to believe, the resurrected saints will arrive with Jesus on the Mount of Olives.

Our physical bodies are not needed in order to be with the Lord in heaven. Old Testament saints have been with Christ for two thousand years without their resurrected bodies. Our resurrected bodies are given to us for the earth, the same way we now live in these perishable bodies while we are here. It is for the earth realm that our souls and spirits need bodies in which to function.

The reason that I believe that the rapture (our gathering together unto Him) and the Second Coming of Christ are one event is to understand the resurrection of our imperishable bodies. They are needed for the completion of our mission, which is not in heaven, but is on the earth. The kingdom of this world has now become the Lord's and ours! I have never understood a rapture that resurrects the saints and then takes us to heaven. We don't need resurrected bodies in heaven.

When does the resurrection occur? According to the gospel of John, it will be on the last day. This message is repeated several times in this gospel (John 6:39,40,44, 54, and 11:24).

The Arrival

Zechariah was given a vision to see the arrival of the Messiah. In Zechariah 14: 1-15, the prophet declares the exact time and place where the Messiah will arrive. The Lord will return after Jerusalem is plundered, women are ravished, and many are exiled by the forces of these nations.

Israel will not suffer total annihilation and expulsion again but will receive a new story. The feet of the Lord will land on the Mount of Olives and split that mountain with a great earthquake that day. His saints also return with Him to form a mighty army that throws confusion into all of the enemy's camp.

Revelation pictures Jesus coming back on a white horse with all of the armies of heaven coming with Him on white horses. In Revelation's apocalyptic style, these white horses represent royalty and authority. Jesus is pictured slaying these armies of the nations with the sword coming out of His mouth. Because of the authority that He carries, He only has to speak, and the armies of the earth will die.

Zechariah 14:12-13 gives us some more details of this day. "Now this will be the plague with which the Lord will strike all the peoples who have gone to war against Jerusalem; their flesh will rot while they stand on their feet, and their eyes will rot in their sockets, and their tongue will rot in their mouth. It will come about in that day that a great panic from the Lord will fall on them; and they will seize one another's hand, and the hand of one will be lifted up against the hand of another."

Revelation describes this day even more. In chapter 14:19-20, an angel swings a sickle to the earth, gathers the vine of the earth, and throws them into the great wine press of the wrath of God. This winepress is trodden outside the city of Jerusalem. Blood comes out of the wine press, up to the horses' bridles, for a distance of two hundred miles. Again, it is hard to fathom the final judgment that awaits the world, just as it is to understand the devastation of the terrible day of the Lord. Both days of judgment will exact a heavy toll of human life, making the inhabitants of the earth scarce.

Daniel and Revelation describe the end of the antichrist ruler. Jesus puts him to death; he is thrown alive into the lake of fire, along with the false prophet. The end of Babylon has finally come. Her long-standing control over nations and people is no more.

The Great Supper

In Revelation, the destruction of this day marks the most victorious triumph for the saints. Judgment now has been passed in favor of the righteous. They have been vindicated on this day, being witnesses to the final destruction of Babylon the Great. This past age, so hostile to them, is now over. This is their day of vindication.

So the Lord will bring the saints to the feast. It is His marriage supper, a consummation feast of the gathering together of His bride and the destruction of her enemies. At this feast, the saints witness the destruction of the flesh of the armies, which are gathered to destroy Jerusalem and Israel. These armies represent all of the nations throughout history that have opposed the rule of Jesus and persecuted His messengers. Israel will never be threatened again.

The coming of the Lord is the hope of the New Testament. The doctrine of an early rapture, which has been embraced for many years, teaches that this marriage supper of the Lamb will be held in heaven. In fact, most people believe that the rapture will take us to heaven to live forever and ever. Unfortunately, the doctrine of an early rapture has replaced the literal coming of the Lord as the hope of believers. Because of this distortion, we misunderstand the end of our destiny. Staying in heaven forever is neither the message nor the hope of the New Testament.

The New Testament teaches just one coming of the Lord. It is in this day that we place our hope. The marriage supper of the Lamb is the feast of the gathering of the bride of Christ and the destruction of her enemies. This day is the Day of Atonement when the Lord destroys wickedness and exalts and vindicates the righteous. Another shadow of this victory was the eighth feast of Israel that was added during the time of Esther. This feast, the feast of Purim, celebrated the overcoming of another antichrist assault by Haman, and the great victory the Jews experienced over their enemies.

The kingdom of this world has now become the kingdom of our Lord and of His Christ. This is the day we have been waiting for since Jesus ascended to heaven. This is the Day of Atonement, when evil is delivered a final blow, and the Lord vindicates the righteous.

The marriage supper of the Lamb will not last long. This battle is uneven in its balance of power. The last battle of man will not be between nations, but between the forces of righteousness and the forces of evil. Once the battle is over, Israel must meet her Messiah.

Chapter Eight
REVEALING MESSIAH

Zechariah 12:10 – "I will pour out on the house of David and on the inhabitants of Jerusalem, the Spirit of grace and of supplication, so that they will look on Me whom they have pierced; and they will mourn for Him, as one mourns for an only son, and they will weep bitterly over Him like the bitter weeping over a firstborn."

Though Israel is saved from destruction on the day of the Lord, she has not gone unpunished. The day of her distress is a difficult time of testing and refining (Malachi 3:1-3). Jerusalem has once again been humbled.

Try to imagine Israel's position. Just hours ago, her enemies surrounded her, encamped on all sides, poised to destroy her completely. Some of the armies began to purge the city, ravishing the women, wreaking havoc everywhere. The hopelessness of that hour is unbearable.

Then it happens. There is a great earthquake at the sound of a trumpet. In the sky above, someone is leading a charge of an innumerable heavenly host. The armies ravishing the city are stopped dead in their tracks.

After taking care of the forces in the city, this heavenly host heads to the valley of Armageddon to confront the rest of the armies. Later that same day, they return to Jerusalem. Deep inside, Israel knows that her Messiah has come.

We don't know when Jesus will reveal Himself to them. Perhaps it is immediately after He stops the ravishing of the city of Jerusalem. Perhaps, when they all return from Armageddon, He will go before His army and reveal Himself then. At some point on this day, Jesus will reveal Himself to Israel.

According to Zechariah, a spirit of grace and supplication will be poured out on the inhabitants of Jerusalem. When the Messiah returns, they will look on Him whom they pierced and weep in utter brokenness. This day will be a day of great mourning, but not over their annihilation, as they had feared. The people of Israel are absolutely broken over the revelation that Jesus, the One whom they had crucified, is their Messiah.

It will be so humbling for Israel to accept this revelation. After rejecting His love for over two thousand years, they will fall to the ground with great weeping. In utter brokenness, they will mourn by themselves trying to cope with this reality. They are probably a little frightened over what they think may happen next.

But the judgment is finally over. The seven years of torment seemed like a hundred and caused so much havoc in such a short period of time. According to Isaiah, the people left on the earth are scarcer than pure gold (Isaiah 13:12). The army of believers resurrected and gathered with Christ will probably be a great majority in that day.

The Victory Parade

We don't know when many of these scriptures will be fulfilled, but we know that they all will come to pass. There are several old songs that we used to sing in the 1980's that surely will find their fulfillment on or soon after this day.

"Therefore the redeemed of the Lord shall return and come with singing unto Zion, and everlasting joy shall be upon their heads. They shall obtain gladness and joy; and sorrow and mourning shall flee away!" (Isaiah 51:11)

"For you will go out with joy and be led forth with peace, the mountains and the hills will break forth into shouts of joy before you, and all the trees of the fields will clap their hands." (Isaiah 55:12)

"O clap your hands, all peoples; shout to God with the voice of joy. For the Lord Most High is to be feared, a great King over all the earth. He subdues peoples under us and nations under our feet. For God has ascended with a shout, the Lord with the sound of the trumpet. Sing praises to God, sing praises. Sing praises to our King, sing praises. For God is the King of all the earth; sing praises with a skillful psalm. God reigns over the nations, God sits on His holy throne. The princes of the people have assembled themselves as the people of the God of Abraham, for the shields of the earth belong to God; He is highly exalted." (Psalm 47:1-3 and 5-9)

The journey from Megiddo to Jerusalem winds through the hills of Judea. The saints of all time will come marching through those hills and into Zion. Many, especially the Old Testament saints, had seen this day from afar and longed for its fulfillment. But sprinkled in the midst of patriarchs and saints from ages past, are people who just hours ago survived some of the most horrid conditions on earth. Yet in a moment, in a twinkling of an eye, they were changed, caught up to meet the Lord in the air. With resurrected bodies, they have joined the saints in witnessing the greatest victory ever, the war that literally ended all wars. Now, they are marching into Zion. Imagine the rejoicing!

The earth has also longed for this day. For the earth herself has been subject to futility and has experienced every weapon that man could devise against her. She also endured every judgment that the Lord poured out against her inhabitants. Even the earth will rejoice in this day, to see the revelation of the sons of God (Romans 8:20-22).

The earth is done groaning. On this day, she can't help herself. The mountains and the hills of Judea shout for joy, and even the trees of the field clap their hands. The Messiah has returned to the earth and restoration is at hand!

When the saints return to Jerusalem, they encounter the inhabitants weeping and crying over the revelation of Jesus as their Messiah. This repentance is foreshadowed in the Old Testament during the time of Nehemiah. I believe what happened then, will happen again on this day.

The Feast of Tabernacles

In the book of Nehemiah, the people of Jerusalem just experienced a miraculous deliverance. In less than two months, the walls of Jerusalem were rebuilt, making the city secure from their enemies. On the first day of the seventh month, they gathered at the square, which was in front of the Water Gate, and Ezra, the priest, began to read the scroll of Moses. As he read, a spirit of grace and supplication fell on the people who began to weep uncontrollably – the same spirit that will fall on Israel at the revelation of their Messiah.

What did Nehemiah and the leaders do when that happened? They did what I believe the saints of God will do upon arriving in Jerusalem on that day. Nehemiah sent the Levites out into the people to tell them that this day was holy unto the Lord, "Do not grieve," they told the people, "For the joy of the Lord is your strength."

After Nehemiah calmed the people, they went away and prepared a great feast, the feast of the Tabernacles, and served it to the governor and the priests. They understood the great revelation of their day. The Lord of heaven and earth is now dwelling with man. So it will be on the day of the Lord when He returns.

> "The Lord of hosts will prepare a lavish banquet for all peoples on this mountain; a banquet of aged wine, choice pieces with marrow, and refined, aged wine. And on this mountain, He will swallow up the covering, which is over all peoples, even the veil which is stretched over all nations. He will swallow up death for all time, and the Lord God will wipe tears away from all faces, and He will remove the reproach of His people from all the earth. For the Lord has spoken. And it will be said in that day, 'Behold this is our God for whom we have waited; let us be glad and rejoice in His salvation.'" (Isaiah 25:6-9)

The terrible time of the judgment season of the day of the

Lord has been brought to an end, in one day, just like it began. The judgment is over; the banquet has begun, the great feast of Tabernacles. The precious blood of the Lamb and of the saints has been vindicated by the judgments of the Lord. Believers are all together now, celebrating, getting to know each other. Loved ones are reacquainted; saints are meeting old friends and new ones and sitting with the giants of our faith in Jerusalem, upon the mountain of our God. It is a time of great celebration and joy. Jesus spoke of this table when He was here. (Matthew 8:11, Luke 22:30)

Contemplating These Truths

If I've wrecked your theology by writing this book, I can't apologize. I know that most of you think that this was all going to happen in heaven. Most believe we are going to stay there for all eternity. It is time to read the Bible, putting off speculations and reading what the Bible clearly teaches. The righteous shall inherit the earth.

I know that these first eight chapters might have shaken you to the core. Maybe you won't want to share this book with a friend because you are afraid it will frighten them; I understand. However, do you want their blood to be on your hands? Will we, who know the truth about the day of the Lord, keep silent and watch the world go to this judgment without warning them?

You see, the end of the day of the Lord is much better than its frightful beginning. Paul told us that eye has not seen, and ear has not heard, and things which have not entered the heart of man, God has prepared for those who love Him (I Corinthians 2:9). The Bible gives us even more glimpses of the age to come.

All of the New Testament commands us to get ready for the

coming of the Lord. We are invited to be in Jerusalem and to sit with Abraham at the table of the kingdom of God. But just as Jesus warned His own people during His first stay here on earth, there is also a place of torment and great gnashing of teeth for the unfaithful who have lived their lives in rebellion to His Lordship.

If you have never given your heart to the Lord, I beg you to consider doing that right now. Repent of your sins, and find a church to help disciple you in the Lordship of Jesus. There is a place waiting for you at this table. You are invited and welcome at the table of the kingdom of God.

THE DAY

PART 4:

THE DAY OF THE LORD— JESUS' RULE AND REIGN

Chapter Nine
THE THRONE OF JESUS— EZEKIEL'S TEMPLE

Malachi 3:1 – "And the Lord, whom you seek, will suddenly come to His temple; and the messenger of the covenant, in whom you delight, behold, He is coming, says the Lord of Hosts."

Will there or won't there be another temple built in Jerusalem during the last days in preparation for the coming of the Messiah? Will the Messiah build a temple when He comes, like Zechariah says He will? (Zechariah 6:12)

Those who argue against it do so because they believe that Jesus is the fulfillment of everything – the sacrifice, offering, and the temple. It is because He fulfilled them all that there is no need again for any of them.

I believe that two more temples will be built in Israel. The first will be built according to the pattern of the first two temples of Israel, Solomon's temple and Herod's temple. Jesus will build the final temple.

Why is there a need for more temples when the New Testament teaches that our bodies are now the temple of God? If the final age on earth was only for the resurrected saints, then I don't think there would be a need for another temple. Jesus fulfills all, for those of us who believe, but what about the unbeliever?

There are going to be unbelievers in the next age. They may not be total unbelievers anymore, for it will be hard to deny God and His Messiah when He is sitting in Jerusalem ruling the earth. However, they won't have what believers have – imperishable, resurrected bodies. Theirs are still subject to death.

There are many scriptures in Ezekiel, Zechariah, and Isaiah that speak of sacrifices, offerings, feasts, and a temple, which is the throne of Jesus. Many of you may wonder, "Why do we need to shed another drop of animal's blood when Jesus' blood sacrifice paid it all, once and for all?" I will never deny the sacrifice of Jesus or what He did for you and me. We need to add nothing to it, depending solely on His sacrifice for our salvation.

Yet, there are people during this time who will still sin, who will multiply and replenish the earth for the next thousand years. They will enjoy greater benefits than we did in this age because the curse will be lifted from the earth. This current age has been given for salvation, not the next one.

For this reason I believe there will be a temple. The survivors will bring sacrifices and offerings to this place of atonement. Jesus will reign from this place as both Priest and King.

I believe that the survivors and their descendants will live the entire thousand-year reign of Christ being confronted and reminded often of the finished work of Christ. Just as the Old Testament temple was a shadow looking ahead to Christ's sacrifice, this temple will point back to Jesus' intercession and sacrifice. The people who survive and remain will still sin and need atonement, correction, and instruction; they will continue to experience death.

There will be priests and Levites who again will function, and some type of sacrifices will be offered, though nothing like Old Testament times. Often, the survivors will be reminded of the sacrifice that was once offered. I don't believe that they will be condemned but merely reminded of the reason they bow their knee to Jesus alone. The King will be present in His temple with the holes in His hands and in His side to instruct them. The saints also will join the survivors in reverence to the King in this temple, though we will not need atonement. It will be a privilege and an honor to come to Him. With great joy, we will come and worship Jesus when He is seated on His throne.

THE DESTRUCTION OF JERUSALEM AT THE RETURN OF JESUS

As I have already stated in this book, I believe that Israel will build a temple at the beginning of the tribulation, but probably not the one that Ezekiel describes in chapters 40 – 47. There are three New Testament references to this third temple. The first two temples have already been destroyed – Solomon's temple in 586 B.C. and the one that the returning Babylonian exiles built (later was expanded by Herod the Great and usually referred to as Herod's temple, which was destroyed in A.D. 70). This third temple will be visited by the antichrist and desecrated by him. But this is not the temple in which the Lord will build His throne.

So what is going to happen to this "tribulation era" temple? The Bible doesn't say for sure. Jesus may tear it down, or it might not survive the terrible earthquake that happens at the coming of the Lord. Much of Jerusalem will be destroyed in this earthquake. Other major changes will happen to the hills and valleys around Jerusalem and also around the world. Listen to what the scriptures say about this event.

> "Then the seventh angel poured out his bowl upon the air, and a loud voice came out of the temple from the throne, saying, "It is done." And there were flashes of lightning and sounds and peals of thunder; and there was a great earthquake, such as there had not been since man came to be upon the earth, so great an earthquake was it and so mighty. The great city was split into three parts." (Revelation 16:17-20)

> "Then the Lord will go forth and fight against those nations, as when He fights on a day of battle. In that day His feet will stand on the Mount of Olives, which is in front of Jerusalem on the east; and the Mount of Olives will be split in its middle from east to west by a very large valley, so that half of the mountain will move toward the north and the other half toward the south. Then, the Lord, my God, will come, and all the holy ones with Him!" (Zechariah 14:3-5)

There will be a very powerful earthquake when Jesus comes back; it will change the landscape as well as devastate much of the city of Jerusalem. Why would the Lord do this? I believe that much of our work in the millennial kingdom will consist of rebuilding the earth the way Jesus wants it done. Why would He want to come back to a temple that is an Old Covenant temple? As you will see, the temple that Ezekiel measured was not anything like any of the prior temples.

A Unique Temple

The temple which the Lord showed to Ezekiel, has never been built. Zechariah prophesied that the Lord Himself will oversee and be the builder of this temple.

Zechariah 6:12-13 says, "Then say to him, 'Thus says the Lord of hosts, behold, a man whose name is Branch, for He will branch out from where He is; and He will build the temple of the Lord. Yes, it is He who will build the temple of the Lord, and He who will bear the honor and sit and rule on His throne. Thus, He will be a priest on His throne, and the counsel of peace will be between the two offices."

Verse 15 states something that would have never taken place in prior times in Israel. "Those who are far off will come and build the temple of the Lord." Only in Christ is there no longer a distinction between the Jew and Gentile. Jesus will hire or command Gentiles or "a far off" people to build this temple.

Though it is built with chambers for priests, and priests will serve in the temple, there are many differences from the prior temples. First, there is no longer the position of the High Priest, no veil of separation, and no ark of the covenant. Almost all of the furnishings within this temple are completely different from the previous ones. The sacrificial altar is raised up, very large and square, and is no longer approached from the south, as it was previously, but from the east through a set of stairs.

Those priests ministering to the people are those who have been unfaithful in their pasts. In the former years, priests considered it an honor to minister to the people. Now they are commanded to attend to the sacrifices of the people *because* of their previous unfaithfulness. They are not allowed to be a priest to Jesus nor are they given access to Him.

The sons of Zadok, faithful priests, shall attend to the Lord. They will attend to the King/Priest personally. They are granted access into the "nave," which is also called the Holy Place.

This nave appears to be the throne room of Jesus. It is elevated and accessed through stairs, more west of the sacrificial altar. Instead of a Holy of Holies where the Ark of the Covenant sat, there is now a Holy place where the King reigns. There is limited access to Him. This place will become the center of Jerusalem and the center of the entire earth.

Another unique feature of this temple is the river originating just south of the sacrificial altar, trickling out of the east side of this temple. The further you go east in this river, the deeper it gets, as it flows down the mountains that surround Jerusalem toward the Dead Sea. On the bank of this river grow fruit trees, which bear fruit every month due to the water that originates from the sanctuary. Their leaves are also used for healing.

Everything about this temple speaks of Jesus. Of course – He designed it. It is built to exalt who He is and to remind the nations of all that He has done. Both the river of living water and the trees that provide food and healing declare to all His very nature. As the people marry and have more children, as time passes on, representatives of every generation will come and behold this wondrous King and the glorious temple where He dwells.

The Glory of This Place

"For the latter glory of this house will be greater than the former," says the Lord of hosts, "and in this place I will give peace."

The temple that Zerubbabel was building at the time never fulfilled these words. Haggai was looking much further down the road, at another temple and at another time.

Isaiah also got a glimpse of Zion and another unique view of the city during this time. He says in Isaiah 4:2-6,

> "In that day the Branch of the Lord will be beautiful and glorious, and the fruit of the earth will be the pride and the adornment of the survivors of Israel. It will come about that he who is left in Zion and remains in Jerusalem will be called holy, everyone who is recorded for life in Jerusalem. When the Lord has washed away the filth of the daughters of Zion and purged the bloodshed of Jerusalem from her midst, by the spirit of judgment and the spirit of burning, then the Lord will create over the whole area of Mount Zion and over her assemblies a cloud by day, even smoke, and the brightness of a flaming fire by night; for over all the glory will be a canopy. There will be a shelter to give shade from the heat by day, and refuge and protection from the storm and the rain."

This shelter certainly is a reminder to Israel of their journey through the wilderness. It will remind them of how the Lord protected them and will serve as a protective covering over Mt. Zion. The latter glory of this place will truly be great.

Jesus is coming back and will oversee the building of His temple, which is His throne. When the Lord gave Ezekiel a tour of this place, He spoke very clearly to this point. "Son of man, this is the place of My throne and the place of the soles of my feet, where I will dwell among the sons of Israel forever (Ezekiel 43:7)."

The kingship and the priesthood are now one on earth. These two offices are one in Jesus. The temple that Ezekiel measured will serve as a throne and a worship center. Jesus will be exalted in this temple, and intercession will continue all the days of the millennial kingdom. Jesus will rule from this place and make decisions regarding the nations of this world.

Chapter Ten

THE JUDGMENT SEAT OF CHRIST— THE REWARD OF THE SAINTS

II Corinthians 5:10-11 – "For we must all appear before the judgment seat of Christ, so that each one may be recompensed for his deeds in the body, according to what he has done, whether good or bad. Therefore, knowing the fear of the Lord, we persuade men, but we are made manifest to God."

The King and High Priest of our souls will reign soon in Jerusalem. However, these literal fulfillments on earth are nothing new to believers. Jesus has been doing both ministries since the early part of the day of the Lord. In His intercession for mankind, He became not only our Priest; He was also the unblemished sacrifice. When Jesus ascended after His resurrection, He ascended to sit at the right hand of the Father and to begin His reign as King or Lord of heaven and earth. None other than King Jesus has directed the history of the earth during the last two thousand years.

Yet He is also a very merciful High Priest, according to the order of Melchizedek. Melchizedek was not a Jew, but the first known occupier of Jerusalem. He was both a king and a priest. Since Jesus is a priest of his order, He is not just a High Priest for the Jew but also for the Gentile. As recorded in the lineage of Christ, the blood of Gentile women ran through His veins.

Because Jesus came to earth as a man, He understands our weaknesses and our trials. When in brokenness and repentance we turn to Him, He forgives our sin, cleansing us from our iniquities. The New Testament not only declares His Lordship, it also reveals the High Priest interceding for us at the right hand of the Father. The two offices are now one in Jesus the Messiah.

As King, Jesus has had to make tough decisions and judgments. All throughout the last two thousand years, Jesus installed rulers and judged others, bringing the history of man to its final culmination in the day of the Lord. He is sovereign, yet merciful.

Will the millennial temple be built before Jesus sits as a judge? I have no idea the exact order of these events. It seems reasonable that the temple will be built so that Jesus can make judgments from His throne. I simply wanted to address the fact that the temple will be built by Gentiles, and will illustrate to the world that the offices of king and priest are now one in Christ. The throne of Jesus is in this temple.

During the reign of King Jesus, He will make many judgments and decisions. Isaiah 2:4 says, "And He will judge between the nations, and will render decisions for many peoples." As Jesus prepares His kingdom for the rebuilding of the earth, He will decide the greatness and the scope of the nations or various lands of the earth.

Many of these judgments are already written in the Word. Old nations such as Egypt, Syria, and Edom have edicts pronounced for and against them because of how they treated God's people in the last age. Their greatness in this age will be determined by their past faithfulness or unfaithfulness.

There are also judgments handed down to govern the whole of society. Isaiah tells us that decisions will be made for peoples far and wide. He then gives us a glimpse of one of these decisions – no longer will nations be allowed to lift up a sword against another nation. Never again will men learn war.

Other decisions will be made. For example, a highway running from Egypt, through Israel, and all the way into Syria will be built. Today, border walls of strife and animosity separate these peoples, who guard their territories with guns and weapons. It will not be that way during the reign of King Jesus. The Highway of Holiness will be its name and will join lands together that have lived separately all throughout the Babylonian age.

Jesus will sit as judge for the poor and the impaired. Is any one blind? Not in Jesus' kingdom, neither will there be any deaf or lame people. The tongue of the mute will speak and will shout for joy! Places that earlier were deserts, will now have streams running through them and will spring forth with life. Jesus will speak and render these decisions, and it will be so.

Jesus will also make decisions regarding animals and the earth. No longer will any animals prey on each other or mankind. Listen to what Isaiah declares about this glorious hour.

> "And the wolf will dwell with the lamb, and the leopard will lie down with the young goat, and the calf and the young lion and the fatling together; and a little boy will lead them. Also the cow and the bear will graze, their young will lie down together, and the lion will eat straw like the ox. The nursing child will play by the hole of the cobra, and the

weaned child will put his hand on the viper's den. They will not hurt or destroy in all My holy mountain, for the earth will be filled with the knowledge of the Lord as the waters cover the sea. And in that day the nations will resort to the root of Jesse, who will stand as a signal for the peoples; and His resting place shall be glorious." (Isaiah 11:6-10)

There are many judgments and decisions that will be made for nations, peoples, lands, and animals. But, there is another day in the day of the Lord. It is the day when King Jesus will sit on His glorious throne and will judge us as individuals.

THE BEMA SEAT

This individual judgment is described in II Corinthians 5:10. The Greek word for judgment in this verse is the word *Bema*; it refers to a raised step or platform where judges stood or sat to make judgments. A broad range of bema seats existed during Paul's day. Many Jewish synagogues had a Bema seat where the Word of God was read. Courtrooms had a Bema seat where cases were heard and judgments were made, often concerning innocence or guilt. For sporting events, the judges would watch the event or race and make sure that the rules were followed from the Bema seat. The victorious winners were then rewarded at this seat of judgment.

Paul stated several times in his letters that we as believers must be brought before the judgment (bema) seat of Christ. In I Corinthians 3, Paul speaks at length about this judgment, which is based on how we built upon the foundation of Christ in this life. Paul says that our works will be tested by fire. That which remains through the fire will receive a reward.

All that we have sacrificed for Jesus' kingdom will be rewarded that day, as also all that was done selfishly will be burned up. Even the giving of a cup of water to a little one will be rewarded. Every careless word and action will be burned up in the fire.

Early in Jesus' reign, rewards will be given. This is the bema seat judgment – individuals are given rewards and assignments. They will then be sent out to rule the nations and the cities of the earth.

When Jesus was here on earth His followers assumed that Jesus was bringing the kingdom immediately. Jesus told them this story to help them understand His mission.

So He said,

> "A nobleman went to a distant country to receive a kingdom for himself, and then return. And he called ten of his slaves and gave them ten minas and said to them, 'Do business with this until I come back.' But his citizens hated him and sent a delegation after him saying, 'We do not want you to rule over us.' When he returned, after receiving the kingdom, he ordered that these slaves, to whom he had given the money, be called to him so that he might know what kind of business they had done."
>
> "The first appeared, saying, 'Master, your mina made ten minas more.' And he said to him, 'Well done, good slave, because you have been faithful in a very little thing, you are to be in authority over

ten cities.' The second came, saying, 'Master, your mina has made five minas.' And he said to him also, 'And you shall be over five cities.' Another came, saying, 'Master, here is your mina, which I kept put away in a handkerchief; for I was afraid of you, because you take up what you did not lay down and reap what you did not sow."

"He said to him, 'By your own words I will judge you, you worthless slave. Did you know that I am an exacting man, taking up what I did not lay down and reaping what I did not sow? Then why did you not put my money in the bank, and having come, I would have collected it with interest?' Then he said, 'Take the mina away from him and give it to the one who has the ten minas.' And they said to him, 'Master, he has ten minas already.' "

"I tell you that to everyone who has, more shall be given, but from the one who does not have, even what he does have shall be taken away. But these enemies of mine, who did not want me to rule over them, bring them here and slay them in my presence." (Luke 19:12-27)

Many believers regard this only as a simple teaching parable, but I think it reveals much about the bema seat judgment of the believer. The story is completely true. Jesus went away, and while He was away, the nations of this earth declared that they didn't want Him to rule. While He was gone, His servants did business with the gifts that they were given. When He returns, He will call each one of us to give an account for our stewardship of His gifts to us.

Some earnestly labored and were very fruitful, so they will be rulers of nations (ten cities). Some will be governors, ruling over five cities. Some won't rule at all, but will serve wherever Jesus places them. They have no fruit at all which the Bema judgment reveals.

This particular judgment doesn't determine eternal salvation; that has already been decided in our gathering together unto the Lord and in our new, imperishable bodies. Those who didn't want Him to rule over them likewise have been given over to judgment on the terrible day of the Lord. This Bema judgment determines our standing in His kingdom, by the number of crowns we wear, and by the cities we will rule over.

One day your name will be called, and you will face the judgment seat of Christ. The believer's judgment will be first, and our rewards – or lack of them – will be revealed. You and I will bear our glory or lack of it for a thousand years to come.

The King and Priest will return, and He is one. As King, He rules and makes the difficult decisions. As Priest, He understands our weaknesses and is merciful to us. None of us deserve any reward. How would any of us stand on that day without His priesthood? But stand we will, for the Lord is able to make us stand (Romans 14:4).

Think about the love and mercy evident in His first edicts—no more war, no more sickness, and animals will no longer hurt us or each other any more. Who wouldn't want to live in that world? Who wouldn't want that King to be Lord over us? The truth is – this is who He is now; this is whom we are submitted to in this age. This is our Lord, our King, and our Priest!

> "So that at the name of Jesus, every knee will bow, of those who are in heaven and on earth and under the earth, and that every tongue will confess that Jesus Christ is Lord, to the glory of God the Father." (Philippians 2:10-11)

At the Bema Seat, resurrected saints will be rewarded for past faithfulness. It is sobering to think of meeting Jesus face to face at this judgment seat. I don't believe we will account for our sins or mistakes, but for how we lived our lives in service for Him. We will have to look into His eyes and feel them piercing through our very souls. It is the "Well done, good and faithful servant" that we all want to hear. Let us finish this race well and prepare ourselves for the hour that awaits us.

Though the Bible doesn't say much about those who are found fruitless, it is obvious from the story that the Lord isn't very pleased with them. Though they are not destroyed, neither will they wear any crowns. They will probably serve much in the same way that the unfaithful priests will serve in the Temple of God.

I don't know if you are satisfied with your fruit offering to the Lord, but I certainly am not. In faith, I am believing the Lord for the greatest season of reaping that I have ever experienced in my ministry. I don't want to go before the Lord empty-handed and experience shame on that day. Everything inside of us wants to hear, "Well done, good and faithful servant!" We all want to have a great part in the rebuilding of the earth and the exalting of our King in Israel.

As believers, it is not the fate of our salvation that will be decided at the Bema seat of judgment, but our destiny to rule, reign, or serve. How we labor in this hour will determine our rewards or lack of them. Let us wake up and be busy in the kingdom of our God during the short time that we have left on this earth. Like our sports heroes, let's lay it all out on the field of this life, saving nothing, for the time is short. The Bema seat judgment awaits every believer.

Chapter Eleven

ISRAEL'S GLORY AND PRINCE DAVID

Ezekiel 34:29-30 – *"I will establish for them a renowned planting place, and they will not again be victims of famine in the land, and they will not endure the insults of the nations anymore. Then, they will know that I, the Lord their God, am with them and that they, the house of Israel, are My people," declares the Lord God.*

Ezekiel 34:23-24 – *"Then I will set over them one shepherd, My servant David, and he will feed them; he will feed them himself and be their shepherd. And I, the Lord, will be their God, and My servant David will be prince among them; I the Lord have spoken.*

One **of the main themes of the day of the Lord is the restoration of Israel.** The end time's clock begins to tick, when the Lord gathers the scattered Jewish people and brings them into the land. The prophetic fulfillment of their gathering as a nation is the clearest sign that the times of the Gentiles will soon be fulfilled and that the day of the Lord is at hand. God has planned this strictly according to His eternal purpose and His mercy.

Let's review some of the prophetic words that have been spoken over this nation and events leading to the coming of their Messiah – and ours.

- Ezekiel 36 and 37 prophesies Israel becoming a nation again, and the step by step rebuilding of this nation is given to Ezekiel in a vision of the valley of dry bones. God promises in the prophets that after they are gathered together again, Israel will never lose this land, although He will still punish them, with some being exiled from the land. However, these chastisements don't include Israel's total expulsion from the land as in previous judgments.

- On the day of deliverance, northern nations come to take their land, but the Lord intervenes and saves Israel (Ezekiel 38 and 39). Though they are largely a secular nation now, this day will call the Jews back to their Old Testament roots.

- Following the terrible day of the Lord, Israel will lose all of her allies, and the day of Jacob's trouble will begin. The last seven years of this age will reveal Israel in conflict with the antichrist, a ruler over most of the remaining nations of the world.

- At the end of the age, the antichrist will gather all nations together to the large valley of Armageddon and begin a raid on Jerusalem. His desire is to annihilate Jerusalem and the entire nation of Israel. Jerusalem will be raided and ravished on that day, but that will be the end of her punishment. Her Savior and King will return and deliver her.

All of these prophetic events occur because of God's great love for Israel, despite Israel's rejection of her Messiah two thousand years ago. All the nations of the world will be brought to judgment at the end of the age, including Israel, who will not be destroyed, but who will not go unpunished either. As the nations plan again her total annihilation, Jesus her Deliverer will return. The faithful bride also returns on that day having received their resurrected bodies and having been invited to the marriage supper of the Lamb.

We have already documented the day of the Lord's return. The weeping and mourning of that day in Israel will not be over the judgment, but over the clear revelation of who is their Messiah. When they realize what they have done and how they have rejected Him, they will be broken and overcome with intense grief. They will grieve alone that day, until the Lord comes back from Armageddon and wipes the tears away from their eyes. It is my guess that these grateful people will serve the feast of the Tabernacles that the Lord has prepared for His bride, just as the weeping people of Nehemiah prepared and served the feast to Nehemiah (the governor) and the priests.

After this feast is over, it will be time to rebuild the earth. It is apparent in all the scriptures that this will begin in Israel. Zechariah and Ezekiel prophesy a temple to be built under the direction of Jesus, and serve as the worship center and His throne. He will employ Gentiles to build this temple.

In the rebuilding phase of Israel, land will be apportioned

again to the Jews. In Ezekiel 47 and 48, Israel is apportioned the original territory that Abraham was promised in Genesis 15. To this date, Israel has never owned or occupied all of this territory (from the Nile River to the River Euphrates). I believe all resurrected Jews will receive their inheritance, as once again, each of their tribes is given their portion of land. There is also a large portion to be given to the prince of Israel. We already know who that honor will be bestowed upon.

David's Honor

Who but King David merits the honor of rebuilding the city of Jerusalem and the nation of Israel? David's passion for God is well documented in the Word – so also are his sins. Many believers in the church have belittled his character and his accomplishments because of those sins. But a thousand years before Jesus came, David seemed to possess an understanding of the gospel. He, like Paul, recognized himself as the chief sinner who was in need of the mercy of God. He was given the great revelation that his sins were forgiven, as Psalms 32 and 51 declare.

My last book, *The Place*, outlines the role David played in discovering the place where God chose to establish His name. David was the Jewish founder of the city of Jerusalem. He discovered the exact place where God chose to establish His name, which had been left vacant of the ministry of God since the days of Melchizedek, king and priest of Salem.

It was David who built the city and established it as the capital city, not just in government, but also as the worship center for Israel. He brought together the scattered Levitical priests and ordered the unceasing ministry of the worship of the Lord in Zion. Although he was a mighty conqueror, he never neglected the ministry of the Lord in Zion. He built storehouses of provision for the priests so they could minister night and day at the tent of meeting. David knew where his strength and help came from. Israel has not known such a time of prosperity, peace, and security since the days of the latter end of his rule and the early part of his son's reign.

But that will change when Jesus returns.

Certainly there were other wonderful choices for this position of the prince of Israel. Noah, Daniel, and Job all seem to be in God's hall of fame for human righteousness (Ezekiel 14:14, 20). I am sure they will be held in high esteem in the resurrection and will be given great rewards, yet they were not chosen to be the prince of Israel. (Noah and Job weren't even Israelites.) Abraham may also have been a great choice – after all, wasn't he the father of Israel and the father of our faith? All of the blessings in this world came through him and his faith. Yet he was not chosen to be the prince.

Moses was esteemed higher than any other Patriarch by the Jews of Jesus' day. He gave them the law and somehow led millions of Jews through the terrible wilderness. He was faithful in the midst of a very unfaithful generation of Israelites. Yet he was not chosen as the prince of Israel. David was chosen above them all.

Jesus and David have a mysterious relationship. You see, Jesus is actually of David's lineage and was known as the son of David. Jesus is both David's son, and His Lord. David, on the other hand, saw Jesus' day and prophesied about His death and resurrection. David also declared that His Lord would return to the Father and sit down until His enemies became the footstool for His feet.

In the resurrection, Jesus and David will rule together over Israel, one as King and the other as His prince. They will cause Israel to rise to the highest of heights and to her greatest glory. All of the prophets saw this day.

> "I will establish for them a renowned planting place, and they will not again be victims of famine in the land, and they will not endure the insults of the nations anymore. Then they will know that I, the Lord their God, am with them, and that they, the house of Israel, are my people," declares the Lord God. (Ezekiel 34:29-30)

> "Now it will come about that in the last days the mountain of the house of the Lord will be established as the chief of the mountains, and will be raised above the hills; and all the nations will stream to it. And many peoples will come and say, "Come and let us go up unto the mountain of the Lord, to the house of the God of Jacob. That He may teach us concerning His ways, and that we may walk in His paths." For the law will go forth from Zion and the word of the Lord from Jerusalem." (Isaiah 2:2-3)

> "'Behold, I am going to deal at that time with all your oppressors, I will save the lame and gather the outcast, and I will turn their shame into praise and renown in all the earth. At that time, I will bring you in, even at the time when I gather you together; indeed, I will give you renown and praise among all

the peoples of the earth, when I restore your fortunes before your eyes,' says the Lord." (Zephaniah 3:19-20)

"Then the sovereignty, the dominion and the greatness of all the kingdoms under the whole heaven will be given to the people of the saints of the Highest One; His kingdom will be an everlasting kingdom and all the dominions will serve and obey Him." (Daniel 7:27)

"Behold, the days are coming," declares the Lord, "When I will raise up for David a righteous Branch; and He will reign as king and act wisely and do justice and righteousness in the land. In His days Judah will be saved, and Israel will dwell securely; and this is His name by which He will be called, 'The Lord our righteousness.' Therefore behold days are coming," declares the Lord, "when they will no longer say, 'As the Lord lives who brought up the sons of Israel form the land of Egypt,' but, 'As the Lord lives who brought up and led back the descendants of the household of Israel from the north land and from all the countries where I had driven them.' Then they will live on their own soil." (Jeremiah 23:5-8)

There are many scriptures that announce the heights to which Israel will rise during the days of King Jesus and Prince David. But perhaps the most brilliant of all passages dealing with Israel's supremacy is Isaiah 60. Take some time and read this chapter. It is too long to quote it all. Isaiah received the most powerful of all revelations about this time period. It will be a time of great glory, when nations and kings will serve Israel and bring their wealth to her. No longer will she be hated or despised but instead will bring joy to generation after generation.

What a day it will be when Jesus and David are together, ruling over Israel with righteousness. It will be a day of renown, of Israel's greatest glory. The righteous will inherit the earth, and Israel will reach the zenith of her power and glory.

Jerusalem will also be exalted at this time. Not only will Jerusalem serve as the capital of Israel, it will also become the center of the world. Nations will bring their offerings to her, receive their instructions, and celebrate Israel's feasts. This will not be neglected during the entire thousand-year rule of Jesus. Israel will be foremost among all the nations, and Jerusalem will be adorned and exalted in righteousness.

A great day of deliverance, health, and healing is coming to the nation of Israel. It is a promise that God gave to the early fathers, and He will bring this promise to fulfillment (Micah 7:20). Jesus and David will lead this restoration time. All nations will be subject to Israel who will rise to a place of renown during the reign of Jesus. Nations will live in shame, remembering the way they previously acted, developing the weapons that caused so much havoc in the world (Micah 7:16-17). They will now be subjected to the nation of Israel and to the King and prince who reign from Mount Zion.

During my lifetime, Israel has become a nation and risen quickly to power and great might. This nation is being prepared for the coming of Messiah. Israel will suffer greatly in the years to come, but a remnant will survive and receive Messiah when He returns. His final reign and kingdom will be glorious at the place where God chose to establish His name. Israel will fulfill the mission that the Lord had given her from the foundation of her calling, and David will be her prince and lead this great restoration in the day of the Lord.

> "Arise, shine, for your light has come. And the glory of the Lord has risen upon you. For behold, darkness will cover the earth, deep darkness the peoples. But the Lord will rise upon you. And nations will come to your light, and kings to the brightness of your rising." (Isaiah 60:1-3)

Chapter Twelve

THE RESTORED EARTH— REBUILDING THE RUINS

Isaiah 61:4 – "Then they will rebuild the ancient ruins, they will raise up the former devastations. And they will repair the ruined cities, the desolations of many generations."

Isaiah 65:20-23 – "No longer will there be in it an infant who lives but a few days, or an old man who does not live out his days; for the youth will die at the age of one hundred and the one who does not reach the age of one hundred will be thought accursed. They will build houses and inhabit them; they will also plant vineyards and eat their fruit. They will not build and another inhabit, they will not plant and another eat; For as the lifetime of a tree, so will be the days of My people, and My chosen ones will wear out the work of their hands, they will not labor in vain, or bear children for calamity; for they are the offspring of those blessed by the Lord, and their descendants with them."

The Bema seat will determine the scope and realm of the rule of believers. Saint after saint will walk in, have his prior life examined and evaluated, and then be given their marching orders. They will be in charge of rebuilding cities and regions of the earth. They, together, will form the government of this kingdom, which rests upon the shoulders of Jesus.

CITIES REDEFINED

It has been a blessing for me to have visited Israel. As I examined the ruins of Bethsaida, near where the Sermon on the Mount was given, I was surprised at how small this city was. I grew up on a farm in rural Southwest Pennsylvania, just outside of a small village. What I call a village, the Bible often calls a city.

Today, we don't call a place a "city" unless there are many thousands of people living in that area. I make this point because of this question: how many saints will there be at the Bema seat? According to John (Revelation 7), the Jews were countable, but the multitudes from every tribe and nation were uncountable.

How many cities are there on the earth? If every little village is a city, they, too, are uncountable. There will be plenty of places to rule. It will be great joy for us saints on Bema seat day when Jesus announces our reward.

HEAVEN?

How many of us who responded to the gospel have been told that heaven is our goal? Heaven is the place where God's throne is; it is also the place of angels, cherubim, and of course, it is the place where Jesus rules today. The Old Testament saints are there, and so are those who have died in Christ. But staying in heaven and living there for all eternity is not the truth of the gospel of the kingdom of God.

If heaven is our goal, then don't you think that the prophets would have given us revelation about our lives there? The prophets all proclaim the same message; there is a great day of restoration when Israel and the entire earth will be restored.

We aren't staying in heaven. Some of us may never see it. Why? Some saints will be alive and remain at the coming of the Lord. According the Apostle Paul in I Corinthians 15, they shall be changed in a twinkling of an eye, and according to I Thessalonians 4, they will be caught up to meet the Lord in the air, and gathered together with all the saints. The Bible never mentions a trip to heaven for these believers. That is inserted by well-meaning people who learned it from other well-meaning people.

It is time for us to study the most neglected part of the Bible, the prophets. The prophets declare the coming Messiah, the restored kingdom, and the effect it will have on the entire earth. Don't we believe the Word of God?

Even after this millennial age, both the earth and the heavens will be burned up. A new earth will be created, and a New Jerusalem will come down out of heaven and be on the new earth. This will be our final abode: New Jerusalem on the new earth.

Preconceived Ideas War Against Truth

The end times aren't really as hard to understand as many think. What makes it hard to understand are all the preconceived ideas that we have. If our goal is going to heaven, then the early rapture becomes the focal point of the end times, because supposedly, this rapture is going to take us to heaven.

But why does Jesus come back, if we are already in heaven? If heaven is the goal, then the restored earth is not. When you read the prophets long enough, you begin to understand the gospel of the kingdom is for the earth. The kingdom already exists in heaven.

The focus of the end times is the return of Jesus to the earth. When you correctly replace the rapture with the true focal point, the return of Christ, then things become so much clearer. The goal of ruling and reigning with Christ on earth becomes our joy – not "going to heaven." If we die before He returns, we will certainly spend time in heaven awaiting our return to the earth. But our goal is to become kings and priests, rulers, and intercessors who will rebuild and rule over the cities and nations of the earth. This end, the Bible says, is glorious. The earth will finally be restored.

Mayors, Governors, Kings, and Priests

At the Bema seat of judgment, territories will be decided; rulers will be assigned. Some of the prior nations will not be represented well and will have their territories reduced because of how they treated God's representatives in this age. Nations will be judged as well as people. Some will get more; others will have less. As I stated before, some of these nations are already judged and their judgment is written down in the prophets.

In a similar way, Jesus will judge us as individuals. According to Luke 19, some may be in charge of ten cities for a job well done in this age, and then be given an eleventh. Some may rule over five cities. Still others may be assigned no cities. What will become of those who don't get a reward because their work all burns up? I believe that they will serve somewhere under the authority of a governor or mayor.

Jesus knows how to reward us for our faithfulness and where to place us righteously as rulers over His earth. His judgments will be the great equalizer for those who suffered greatly in service for Him.

I am very certain that this kingdom will be orderly, that everyone will know who to report to and where to get their orders. Every law and direction will be given from Zion in Israel. All the nations of this world will report to and give an account to Israel. The kings of the earth will be subject to some ruler in Israel – again you can see that there are plenty of positions to go around for Elijah and Elisha, Abraham and Moses, Joseph and Jacob, Peter and John, and the many other saints who will rule and reign with Christ. His kingdom will reign with order and authority.

The Rebuilt Earth

Following the tribulation, the earth will be in great need of restoration. The earth will look much different then in many ways. During the tribulation, islands were swallowed up or moved, mountains were split and brought low. Some were thrown into the sea. The terrain of the earth was changed by the drastic judgments poured out on the nations of the earth. Jesus will also dictate some changes as some deserts will become alive with streams flowing through them, and some previously populated areas will become deserts. The restored earth will be different from the one we know now.

Boundaries will be different because some nations will be abased, while others may have a larger portion. Some cities may never be rebuilt, while others who were small and helpless before might become large and great in His kingdom. (Don't look for Babylon to be rebuilt anytime soon.) The Lord will decide for nations far and wide.

We will build houses, establish these cities, and rule over them. We will outlive our houses and build them again. This is what the prophets have declared will happen. We will also present ourselves to the Lord in Jerusalem at the feast times.

In order to rule over people still subject to sin, there still must be punitive measures. If someone dies under a hundred years old, it will be clear that he was rebellious or accursed. If any nation fails to go up to celebrate the Feast of the Tabernacles, it will not rain on them (Zechariah 14). Never mistake Jesus for a pushover. It will be with great power and authority that He will rule His kingdom. This is symbolized in the Bible with a rod of iron.

Satan Bound

Ruling will mean settling disputes. Sinful people will still cause trouble, but not in the same way or with the same intensity that exists today. We won't be able to settle any disputes with war. Wars are forbidden. We will have to figure it out another way.

Satan with his adversarial ministry will be bound during this season. Think about how much havoc he causes with his mind games. All of this meddling will cease. That doesn't mean sin will cease or that there won't be any trouble. Man is quite capable all by himself.

Jesus' first decisions will find favor with all people. No one will object to the blind being able to see or the lame walking. All people will fall in love with the One we believers already love. Satan's ministry will no longer blind them. Finally, they will see Jesus as He really is.

But, sinful man will still need to be ruled over. We will all have to make tough decisions backed by the authority of our King in Jerusalem. Pastors, if you think ruling a church is difficult (and it most certainly is), what will it be like when we judge angels and rule cities?

What will the restored earth look like? Houses will be built, and then they will wear out and need to be built again. Vineyards will be planted, and every man will have his own. Children will play with animals; animals that used to devour each other will lie down together in the same field. They will neither hurt nor destroy. There will be nothing that will make us afraid any more. As mayors, governors, princes, and kings, we will rule in the next age, or if we have no fruit at all to present to Jesus, we will serve. Welcome to the kingdom of our Lord!

There is so much speculation about what heaven will be like. Do you know why we speculate? Our only revelation of heaven is in Revelation, where John was sent on the day of the Lord. John received glimpses of the judgments poured out to the earth from heaven, and saw the bride getting ready for the return of Jesus. Even Revelation declares the intentions of the Lord to judge, purify, and then restore the earth. The New Testament doesn't change the story; it only makes it clearer than it was in the Old. Now we know who the Messiah is, and that He must rule from heaven until His enemies are made a footstool for His feet.

We are now His witnesses. We must also warn mankind of the coming terrible day of the Lord. Perhaps many will come to their senses, repenting of their idols and of their immoral lifestyles. Ruling and reigning doesn't just begin in the next life; we are practicing every day and auditioning for the positions in that glorious kingdom of heaven. May the Lord find us all faithful.

The earth is groaning now, waiting for the revelation of the sons of God. When we are revealed and sent out, the earth will be restored to a new beauty and freedom from its prior curse.

The earth will be full of the knowledge of the Lord. Therefore, no matter what position we will hold in that kingdom, we will all be teachers instructing the generations about our Great King who lives in Jerusalem. We will tell them the old, old story, the beginning and the end. We will explain what the "old" world was like and how great and wonderful it is to be a part of Christ's kingdom on earth. And, we will share our testimony of what Jesus has done for us personally. What a day, glorious day that will be!

The earth will be the great recipient of all these blessings. Her curse is finally removed. It is hard to think of the earth being able to feel, but she rejoices, groans, mourns, and suffers. All of these verbs are ascribed to the earth. She is waiting for the day the sons of God are revealed, when finally her curse is lifted. Won't we be shocked the day the mountains rejoice and the trees of the field clap their hands! Jesus, the restorer, will restore the earth to her greatest glory since the days before the fall of man.

Chapter Thirteen
SATAN'S FINAL STAND

Revelation 20:7-8 – "When the thousand years are completed, Satan will be released from his prison, and will come out to deceive the nations."

It is hard to believe that not everybody will be excited to bow their knee to our King. However, one more great refinement will happen at the end of the millennial age for the mortal people who are alive at that time.

When the glorious age of the Lord dawns, humans will be scarcer than pure gold. It may be possible for all inhabitants of the earth to be gathered in Jerusalem. It is hard to comprehend the depth of the judgment that is coming to this earth very soon. Isaiah says that the Lord is going to exterminate sinners from the earth.

If a third of the earth is reaped in the first day of judgment, what will be left after Armageddon? Seven years separate the two judgment days of the day of the Lord, and they will prove fatal for many. Jesus said that for the sake of the elect, these days would be shortened.

Yet a remnant will survive, both sinners and righteous. The righteous will be gathered with all the saints at the coming of the Lord. A small group of unbelieving people who remain will know both ages; they will be able to compare what it is like to live under this curse and Satan's power, and they also will know what it will be like to be released from it under the Lordship of Jesus. This small group of humbled people will replenish the earth.

Jesus was clear about marriage for the saints after the resurrection. In Matthew 22, the Sadducees, who didn't believe in the resurrection, attempted to catch Jesus by their wile and intellect. They told Him the story of a woman who continually married brother after brother because the men of that family persistently died. They snidely asked Jesus, "Whose wife shall she be in the resurrection?"

Jesus told them they were very mistaken. The resurrected saints will not marry or be given in marriage but "would be like angels in heaven" (Matthew 22:30). There will be no super race of resurrected people. Faithfulness in this life is our only chance to gain immortality.

It is the other group of humbled people, still subject to sin and death, who will multiply and fill the earth in the next thousand years. According to Isaiah, their lifespan will be as long as a tree. One will still be considered a youth at the age of one hundred.

Methuselah, the oldest man who ever lived, died at the age of 969. In the coming age men will live much longer lives. The first generation may die during the millennial kingdom, but the second generation may have representatives at the end of that age. And of course, in the span of a thousand years, there will be many generations to follow.

Our rule may begin in our city or village with the help of

only a family or two, as we begin to rebuild the ruins. We know that the population of the earth will be drastically diminished at the beginning, so we will learn to rule when our city is small.

After a hundred years, we may be ruling a city of hundreds and later thousands. With no adversaries and few adverse conditions, the earth will repopulate very quickly. Our reign will become more difficult as our cities grow, much like it is today. We will teach each generation about Jesus, His great love for us, and we will prepare offerings to take to the feasts when He commands us to appear in Israel. I am also sure that continued help and support will be available from Jerusalem. I don't believe we will be strangers to Jesus, even as the kingdom grows.

It is also possible that the earth will be restored in stages, beginning with Israel. We may all help to rebuild Israel first, then move outward to the Middle East, and then perhaps to our final destinations of ruling over the earth. We can only speculate about how it will be done, but the Bible declares that the whole earth will be filled with the knowledge of the Lord and His glory.

A thousand years of no war, a thousand years of tame animals, and a thousand years where we will wear out the work of our hands – who would not welcome this kingdom? Who would not want to bow their knees to our wonderful Lord and Savior?

The Bible is clear about what can happen to the second generation who hasn't experienced the judgments, the heartache, and the trials of the previous generations. Listen to Judges 2:10-11. "All that generation also were gathered to their fathers; and there arose another generation after them who did not know the Lord, nor yet the work which He had done for Israel. Then the sons of Israel did evil in the sight of the Lord."

As the earth is repopulated, more and more distance will

be between the people and the Lord. Perhaps the entire first generation, humbled through the tribulation, will know the Lord face to face. After that, nations will be asked to come to Jerusalem for the feasts, but probably only representatives from those nations will come, leaving most people to hear of it only through story. The second generation will become the third, and so forth. Most who are alive on the earth at the end of the millennial rule may never have met Jesus, nor will they remember what the former earth was like.

Do not underestimate the ingratitude of our flesh. People who don't know the Lord, even when He reigns on earth, will judge His edicts as "wrong," and will complain about their treatment and how Israel "gets everything." They will have nothing with which to compare their life with the former cursed earth, as we know it.

And we will rule over them.

The Bible speaks of Jesus ruling the nations with a rod of iron (Revelation 2:27). You might find it hard to believe that punitive measures will be needed during this age. Will prisons be built? Will courts of law be established? None of this will surprise me knowing the heart of man. Even though Satan will be bound, we will experience a thousand year period of man's own capacity to sin. He will not have an adversary to deceive him; he will have no excuse for his behavior except his own depravity.

ONE LAST REBELLION

At the end of this age, Satan will be released. This release may follow right after the judgment of the nations, when Jesus sits as a judge and divides the people, the sheep from the goats. Perhaps, after finding out their eternal destiny, the rebellious will gather with Satan for one last try to overthrow the kingdom of Jesus. Even after being chained up for a thousand years, Satan will still believe that he can overthrow the kingdom of Jesus.

Satan will be released to allow him that last opportunity. He will be allowed to deceive nations and gather them together again. All ungrateful, disgruntled people will hear his voice and respond to his call, just like they do today. The Bible says they will number like the sand on the seashore. They will gather for war, in rebellion to Jesus' decree.

These people don't want Jesus to rule over them anymore. Whatever their complaints, whatever they think is "unfair," will be exposed by their rebellion. They will gather again to the area of Gog and Magog and will be ready again to storm the nation of Israel. There is nothing new under the sun.

What will that war be like? You are forgetting that Jesus banned war a thousand years before. There won't be a war. They will come up to the broad plain (again) and against the camp of the saints with every intention of violence. But no war will be allowed, because Jesus said so. Fire will come down out of heaven and consume them all. Satan will be cast into the Lake of Fire for his final judgment.

What will happen to the people who didn't succumb to the deception of Satan and remained faithful to Jesus in the millennial kingdom? I am not sure the Bible clearly answers that question. If you believe the judgment of the nations happens at the end of His reign (Matthew 25:31-46), then those who are on His right hand are invited into eternal life. Perhaps this is true, but none of us can say for sure or know the outcome of those who aren't deceived by Satan. We must allow righteous judgment to be in the hands of the Lord.

Studying the day of the Lord is not only an effort to understand the repeating history of the earth; it is also about understanding our destiny. The meek and the righteous shall inherit the earth. If you want to be immortal, now is the time to make that decision. Now is the time to have rebellion washed out of our hearts by the Spirit of Jesus. Knowing that the Lord is coming back and that His reward is with Him is sobering. It is time to give of our resources to increasing the kingdom of Jesus in this age. Only this age is given to us to repent of our sins and to receive the Lordship of Jesus in order to inherit immortality and many rewards.

Satan is a problem now, but I have chosen to hardly mention him, except for this final judgment at the end of the millennial age. Though we can't ignore him to or be ignorant of his schemes, he is given far too much attention by so many writers of the end times. I pray that this book gives glory to Jesus. He is the center of our attention and His return is our hope. The day of the Lord is His day; let us honor Him and all that He will accomplish during every season of this day.

The Bible teaches us so much about this wonderful day, the day of the Lord. This day is the most prophesied day in the Bible. The Lord has told us of this day, and even warned us of this day. Ignorance of these scriptures is not an excuse. It should never take any of us by surprise.

The millennial age will end with another attack of Satan and the revealing of men's hearts. Their destruction will mark the end of this age. Now it is time to create a new heaven and earth. The old one, even in its restored state, still bears the scars of rebellion.

So the Lord will burn it with fire and destroy it all. He will start afresh with another Jerusalem, descending out of heaven onto a new earth.

There is no end to this story. Those who have gratefully received the Lordship of Jesus will live on through all of eternity and continue to discover God's great love as He dwells in their midst. But, for Satan and all the ungrateful of heart, there will be pain and misery, eternal separation from God and His great love for them.

Satan's Final Stand

THE DAY

PART 5:

PREPARING FOR THE DAY OF THE LORD

Chapter Fourteen
THIS GENERATION

Luke 21:32 – "Truly I say to you, this generation will not pass away, until all things take place."

Matthew 23:35-36 – "So that upon you may fall the guilt of all the righteous blood shed on earth, from the blood of righteous Abel to the blood of Zechariah, the son of Berechiah, whom you murdered between the temple and the altar. Truly I say to you, all these things shall come upon this generation."

Isaiah 24:6 – "Therefore, a curse devours the earth, and those who live in it are held guilty. Therefore, the inhabitants of the earth are burned, and few men are left."

Revelation 18:8,24 – "For this reason in one day her plagues will come, pestilence and mourning and famine, and she will be burned up with fire; for the Lord God who judges her is strong. And in her was found the blood of prophets and of saints and of all who have been slain on the earth."

There is a generation that is either here, or is coming, which will fulfill these scriptures. There was a "this generation" at 722 B.C. when Israel was destroyed by the Assyrians, and one that lived at 586 B.C. when Judah and Jerusalem were destroyed along with Solomon's temple. The generation of Jesus' first appearance didn't pass away until one million were killed and one hundred thousand were taken captive by the Roman army who destroyed Jerusalem in A.D. 70. Truly, this generation didn't pass away until all the judgments that Jesus passed on them took place.

At the end of the age, Israel is not the focus of the judgment; it will fall on all the other nations of this world. "This generation" will be a worldwide generation of people, not just a generation of unbelieving Israelites. As the day of the Lord draws near, the nations of this world will be shaken and dismayed as this generation is warned of the coming judgment.

The establishment of Israel to the coming of Jesus spanned about two thousand years. The times of the Gentiles has reached a similar length. Gentile nations have had the gospel preached to them for the last two thousand years. As the day draws near, Jesus is requiring of them the fruit of His Lordship. Israel has suffered three major destructive judgments – when the Lord required her fruit, she offered Him idols instead. Israel was given the charge of showing forth His character to the world. Instead, she became a people of idol worshippers, profaning the Lord's holy name.

The Gentile nations have repeated Israel's folly. I don't know whether these generations of judgment deserved it more than the previous ones. But when the patience and longsuffering of the Lord is exhausted, one generation is appropriated the judgment. Upon that generation the wrath of God is poured out.

There will be another "this generation." At the end of every age, there is a harvest, and according to the Bible, there will be two – both the righteous and the wicked. God is just in His judgments. He will protect the righteous, while turning over the wicked to judgment.

So it is that "this generation" could very well be our generation. It pains me to say this. Could it be that our generation has been prepared for the slaughter? Could we not pass this yoke to some other generation of people who don't yet exist? After all, we are very good at passing the blame and avoiding responsibility.

I will not anticipate that another generation will be more depraved than mine. This generation is my generation; we have set the table of judgment. We will continue on the path of total destruction unless a spirit of genuine repentance and humility comes. The Lord commanded, through the prophet Joel, that we seek Him in mourning and repentance.

The Case for This Generation

Why do I believe this generation is our own generation? I believe that the day of the Lord is near, very near. James 5 describes the last generation. They are a rich people, storing their treasure in the last days. This generation has lived luxuriously on earth, living lives of wanton pleasure. They have fattened their hearts in the day of slaughter (James 5:1-6).

In Revelation 3, Jesus speaks prophetically to the church of Laodicea warning them of being lukewarm. This church seems not to need anything and is rich and secure. Yet it doesn't know that it is poor, miserable, and wretched. This prophetic word can easily be applied to our generation. Let's look at the overwhelming evidence that marks our generation as "this generation."

THE FIG TREE

In the Luke passage on the end times (Luke 21:20-33), this generation appears to be the one who sees the fig tree put forth her leaves. When we see this event, we will know the season when Jesus will return and will experience all of the warnings and the judgments that precede this day.

I have never read any reputable author or any prophetic man who doesn't agree on this passage of scripture. Everyone agrees that the fig tree is Israel. When Israel put forth her leaves, the end time clock began to tick. Jesus says very clearly in the context of this event, that this generation will not pass away until the events of the end times come to pass.

Several dates could be argued as possibilities for when Israel "put forth her leaves." I have already mentioned that in 1948, Israel became a nation, and in 1967, Jerusalem became the capital again of the nation of Israel. Yet, it wasn't until the 1990's that many Jews returned to their homeland, after the iron curtain came crashing down. Any of these dates could be the fulfillment of "the fig tree putting forth her leaves," but either way, this generation is now upon us.

WICKED GENERATION

Let's turn back the clock a little bit and look at some collective decisions that all nations have made since the 1960's. First of all, we have witnessed an unrealistic arms race. Nation after nation now has nuclear capability and the ability to lay the earth waste.

I will never forget being herded into our school's basement bomb shelters in the 1960's, as these drills prepared us for an attack in a nuclear age. It was a frightening experience when I was young. At that time, only two nations on the earth had that capability. Today, as we draw closer to such an event, we are sleeping and unprepared. These days, we won't even allow ourselves to think of that possibility, even though far more than two nations now possess this capability. We have buried our heads in the sand, believing that nobody will ever push the button that will change the earth in one day. Yet the Bible predicts the other scenario. That day will come like a thief in the night.

Generation in Love with Silver and Gold

The love of money is the root of all evil. *This generation* has perfected man's greedy lusts and is guilty of loving money. My generation is this generation. The banks and the stock markets of this day rule the world and have great control over mankind. They determine our savings, our retirement, our insurances, and every aspect of our financial lives and our security. They have the power to bring nations to their knees. We are sitting on a precarious precipice.

In the search to make money, this generation has been guilty of hiring people, underpaying them, and then firing them, in order to keep the bottom line looking good. In every way, we have fulfilled the prophecy that James wrote about this last generation. Obviously, the Lord is shaking this system. The financial well being of all nations is being judged. The day of luxurious living is about to end.

Generation who Rejected Jesus

"And you will be hated by all nations because of My name (Matthew 24:9)." All nations in this world are choosing to disrespect and reject the Lordship of Jesus. Whether they like it or not, He is the Lord, and they are accountable to Him. He will contend with all of them for their rejection of His Lordship.

Nations all over the world have chosen many paths of the spirit of antichrist. That is why the antichrist will so easily be received. His spirit is already at work in the nations, preparing the way for the man.

Jesus Unwelcome in Educational Centers

Across the globe, Jesus is no longer welcome in the educational field. He was railroaded out of the American public schools in the 1960's. His presence is ridiculed in our nation's universities, even the ones founded and established to promote the gospel. Today, many of these institutions deny their Lord and their Master, and our generation has promoted this apostasy.

This lack of moral compass and the denial of Jesus has spread seeds of unbelief and rebellion to our children and our youth. We are guilty of leading them to destruction by denying the Lordship of Jesus Christ. Even many churches have followed suit, ashamed of the great name of Jesus. Their judgment has been foretold.

Immoral Generation

Throughout the world, we are embracing new standards of morality that no longer are based upon the Lordship of Jesus. Marriage is under siege and disrespected by most all nations. It is becoming heresy in this world to believe that marriage is a covenant relationship between a man and a woman united by the Lord, and holy in His eyes. In every way, the family has been under siege during the days of this generation, so much so that divorce and broken families now are the rule and not the exception. Malachi saw our day and called this generation to repentance in his prophecy.

Our entertainment for the day is inundated with sexual immorality. Even the heroes in our movies today are immoral by past standards. We have given in to sexual lusts of every kind. It is ruling our society.

Our generation has embraced a woman's right to choose an abortion, rather than holding to the sanctity of life and saving the unborn. Millions of unborn children have died in this holocaust, a holocaust started and guarded by this generation.

We have even tried to move age-old foundations and boundaries. We have rewritten history, accusing past generations of wrong. Isaiah clearly saw our generation when he proclaimed that "they will call evil good, and good evil (Isaiah 5:20)." We need to repent of our immorality and our rebellion to the Lordship of Jesus.

The end result is a society that is collapsing with no moral foothold whatsoever. Divorce is commonplace, even rampant in society; many children are fatherless. Homosexuality has come forth with a militant march, denying our Lord's command for families to be fruitful, multiply, and fill the earth. Instead of filling the earth with righteousness, we are guilty of polluting it with immorality and idolatry.

Truly the prophet Isaiah saw a vision of our generation being prepared for judgment. Isaiah 24:5-6 says, "The earth is polluted by its inhabitants, for they transgressed laws, violated statutes, broke the everlasting covenant. Therefore, a curse devours the earth and those who live in it (this generation) are held guilty."

Abraham Lincoln, in defending the justness of God, once stated "every drop of blood drawn with the lash shall be repaid by another drawn with a sword." If God takes one life for every innocent victim of the millions of unborn children who were sacrificed, will He be unjust? If there is a day of reckoning for all sin, then this generation's selfish pursuits will come to a frightful end. Though the Lord will be accused of being unjust for His judgment on the terrible day, this generation does not recognize how collectively wicked we are. Judgment day will come as a complete surprise.

Generation of Idolaters

Has there ever been a generation of people with more toys and gadgets to steal their time and attention? It is hard to have a conversation with anyone or preach a sermon without getting interrupted by a cell phone. Children play computerized games and seem mesmerized by them. Our generation can't wait for the next electronic device, all under the guise that it will somehow improve our lives. This generation has been captured and enslaved by them.

Look at the way our generation idolizes and pays its entertainers and sports heroes. Could past generations ever understand how it is that the richest in our society are those who entertain us, bringing no value whatsoever to the staples of life? Only this generation has perfected this idolatry.

Travel and Knowledge will Increase

Daniel also states that in the last days men will go to and fro about the earth and knowledge will increase (Daniel 12:4). There are so many signs that my generation is "this generation," one would need to be blind to not see how the Lord has prepared this generation for the end time fulfillment of the day of the Lord. It pains me to admit this truth, but admit it I must. It leads me to deep repentance and intercession for my generation.

I could go on and on with my lament, but I won't. What every individual and every nation on earth will be judged by is this: what have we done with the Lordship of Jesus? Have we bowed our knee to Him and embraced His commands? Have we rejected His rule, rejected all that He is and represents? With every decision we make, we either bow our knee to Jesus or reject His Lordship.

Though we were born in this hour, we still have a decision to make. How will we fulfill the Biblical prophecy of this generation? Many in this generation will continue to live out their lives in the most self-centered ways, and the thief will come suddenly to destroy their lives. Others will repent and turn to the Lord.

Perhaps the judgment will tarry and our generation will pass, but I don't think so. The evidence is too overwhelming. On this generation God will pour out His wrath, and they will be guilty of all the blood of innocent people that has ever been spilt on the earth. This generation will meet with the judgment of God.

God will hold this generation accountable and guilty. He will pour out His judgment in one day when the terrible day of the Lord arrives like a thief. Other than the preceding birth pang warnings, this generation will go to judgment totally unaware. It is our job to sound the alarm and blow the trumpet. It is we who must humble ourselves with great repentance and mourning. May God have mercy on our souls.

The Bride Makes Herself Ready

Amazingly, it is also His bride that comes forth during this same generation. Out of the wickedness and the self-centeredness of this wicked generation will arise people who are in love with God and have separated themselves from Babylon's immoral grip. This bride will be cleansed and purified by the pressures of antichrist, and by the same judgment of fire that will destroy the nations. In her lie the power and the presence of Jesus; she will come forth with purity, boldness, and power. In these last days, the bride of Christ will be a lighthouse to the weak who barely escape the snares and the pressures of this world. A bride who has made herself ready will lead them to righteousness.

This bride will also stand the test of fire and have her faith purified by the trials of these last days. Her members are made clean by the tribulation and strengthened to gather the last harvest of the world. They hold to the testimony of Jesus and love not their lives even unto death. It is this bride that Jesus returns to receive.

Jesus made a statement in Luke's gospel that rings inside me. "However, when the Son of Man comes, will He find faith on the earth (Luke 18:8)?" God will bring swift justice for His elect, but in the process, will they continue to believe in Him? Will they fervently pray for their generation, keeping watch for their souls amidst some of the most difficult and trying circumstances ever presented to mankind?

Let's all answer yes, with great resolve, for we are either of this generation or we are of the bride of Christ. The judgment will plainly expose the difference between the righteous saints and the wicked. So let us prepare, let us seek the Lord while it is still day, for behold, night will come. Wise virgins gather oil while they wait for the Lord to return.

One generation of people, this generation, shall bear the iniquity and the judgment of the final days of this age. Upon them, the Bible declares, will fall the guilt of all the righteous blood of innocent people that was ever shed. Their guilt Jesus declared; their judgment awaits. This generation will not escape, but will fall into the hands of the living God.

Chapter Fifteen
PREPARING FOR THE DAY

I Thessalonians 5:4,6 – *"But you, brethren, are not in darkness, that the day would overtake you like a thief in the night. So then, let us not sleep as others do, but let us be alert and sober."*

Matthew 24:45-46 – *"Who then is the faithful and sensible slave whom his master put in charge of his household to give them their food at the proper time? Blessed is that slave whom his master finds so doing when he comes."*

Hebrews 10:24-25 – *"Let us consider how to stimulate one another to love and good deeds, not forsaking our own assembling together, as is the habit of some, but encouraging one another all the more as you see the day drawing near."*

There is a great and terrible day that is coming upon us. It is inevitable; we cannot avoid it, but we can prepare for it.

If you think buying guns, protecting your property, and selfishly hiding your food would honor the Lord in that day, you are sadly deceived. Some who hear this message are preparing in the most foolish, unbiblical ways. Why would we leave the foundation of the Word as we see this day draw near? Shouldn't we prepare exactly how the Lord told us to prepare?

Not Individualism but Community

The Bible is clear that we are to assemble ourselves together as we see this day draw near. We are to stimulate each other to love and good deeds. Jesus warned that these days would cause many people's love to grow cold.

In Thessalonians 5, after warning the church about the coming of the day of the Lord, Paul directs them to appreciate and submit to those who diligently labor among us. If ever the church of the Lord Jesus Christ needs strong leadership, it will be during the troubled times of the final days.

The best preparation for the coming of this day is to stay busy loving our neighbors and helping to meet their needs. How blessed will be the people whom the Lord so finds when He returns!

Proverbs teaches us that a foolish man separates himself. He quarrels against all sound wisdom. Many people today have given up on the church and are no longer gathering together and living in covenant with their brothers and sisters in the Lord. Most of these have given up on the church because they have been injured. Welcome to the fellowship of the saints! Even Jesus was wounded in the house of His friends; so have I been, along with every other saint of God.

True Christianity doesn't promise us isolation from problems. If it did, we would never have to learn how to forgive and bless those who say cruel things against us. The trials of learning to be brothers and sisters in the body of Christ prepare us for the insults of the world. Jesus knew that we would encounter all of this. He purposely put us into the church to grow and mature, both from nurture and adversity. For this same purpose we are placed into families.

When I was growing up, I was fortunate to know a family of very talented athletes. The third youngest brother in that family of seven children would later go on to stardom in the National Football League and lead the New York Giants to a Super Bowl victory. His two older brothers were football stars in their own right and were several years older. They were much bigger and stronger than he was when he was still in high school. The two older brothers used to beat on him and their youngest brother mercilessly when they played football or basketball together. Believe it or not, it was all done in love—well, most of the time.

Surprisingly, these brothers grew up with a very close bond to each other. Jeff discovered later that the beatings he took from his older brothers when he was young only more prepared him for his future calling.

Why are we so surprised by this same truth in the body of Christ? Don't we read the story of Joseph and his brothers? What about how David was treated by Saul and his army? Even in the New Testament, Paul wanted nothing more to do with John Mark, causing a division between Barnabas and Paul for a season. Neither John Mark, Paul, nor Barnabas gave up on the church. John Mark was not only the first to pen a gospel, he also became very useful to Paul in his latter years. What excuse do we have for not forgiving each other and being a committed part of a local body?

All of us need each other. Communities of faith who love one other and help each other and their neighbors will survive the last days. Individuals will never make it through this dark night alone. The pressure will be too great; they will either act like tyrants or faint from the stress of the day. The Lord will not be pleased with this.

I am beginning to prepare the church under my oversight now for the coming of this day. The most important thing we need to do is love each other and our community. This time is so important because it prepares us to forgive, to have faith in God's ability to provide, and to trust in God's ability to protect us from evil. We also need to be gathered in small groups of people in close proximity to where we live. In case of emergencies, the leaders will need to know how to contact each other and where to gather. The early church functioned this way, and we will have to learn how to do this. Communities of faith will see us through the night.

Hearing the Instructions of the Lord

In these covenant communities of faith, we can most clearly discern the voice of the Lord and respond in faith to it. What if our city is the target of judgment and the Lord warns us of it? He may want us to stay and warn people, call them to repentance, and reap the harvest until a certain time. Or, He might call us away to a place of safety. We must learn to hear His voice and to obey. Our lives will depend on this during the last days.

It may also be that our region is a place of safety to which people flee before or after the day of the Lord. Surely, we won't let them be homeless and suffer, will we? As brothers and sisters of the kingdom, we must do all in our power to share our resources with those who are hurting and have become refugees. Whatever we have, we will share and believe God for the necessary provisions for us all. Difficult days lie ahead for all on the face of the earth.

Jesus warned us with examples of men who went through devastating judgments: Noah and Lot. Both of these men were saved from the judgment, but in very different ways.

Noah built an ark of safety, called his generation to repentance, and invited them to join him in this place of safety. Not one person listened and obeyed, other than his own family. The entire world was destroyed during the first days of the flood, while he was saved by his faith and obedience to the word that God spoke to him. Meanwhile, the people kept living their lifestyle right up to the day of judgment when they were all swept away.

Lot had a very different deliverance. The sin of Sodom and Gomorrah was so great that the Lord had to bring judgment. God sent messengers to warn righteous Lot. He was told to leave all of his possessions and was given explicit instructions to flee to the mountains where his family would be safe. His own son-in-laws laughed at him and tried to discourage him and their wives from leaving. They perished in the judgment.

Lot's own wife was unprepared for this day. She couldn't help but turn around to see what was happening to her friends and her possessions. She turned to salt.

Lot was not prepared for the judgment and the devastation that followed. He became depressed and lived in a cave in the mountains with his daughters, who seduced him into fathering their children. Lot and his family, even though they escaped from the initial judgment, were not prepared for it. As a result, they made terrible choices after this day.

What must we do to prepare for the judgment of our day? We must practice hearing from God and obeying His voice. Our obedience today is paving a path of deliverance for tomorrow. Don't think that you can suddenly bring your flesh into submission and obedience. Life simply doesn't work that way. This is the lesson of Lot and his family.

Don't Love the World

As believers, we are constantly warned in the Bible to come out of Babylon and not touch what is unclean. To literally come out of Babylon, we would somehow have to leave every nation of this world. But that isn't really what the Bible is saying.

We cannot love this world or the things in this world. Many have lost their faith while searching for security in this world system. We must repent of our lust for things, money, and any way in which we have built our own security systems outside of trusting in the Lord.

I believe that we only have a short time to invest all of our money, time, and energy into the kingdom of God. Why do I say "all"? It is clear in the end times that the financial system we are under will be brought down on the day of the Lord. Whatever is being saved for after this day will be lost. Paper money may be good for toilet paper or starting fires after the day, but it's not going to buy anything. The only things that will matter will be food and shelter.

Will believers lose their lives trying to protect their money, houses, or possessions? I pray not. It may be this very trial that separates the true believers from the unbelieving. The last days may come down to this very struggle. Why else would Jesus tell us to remember Lot's wife?

Ezekiel states that people will throw their gold and silver into the streets because it doesn't satisfy their appetite. God is going to take the first world nations and humble them to the level of third world countries, or perhaps worse. The faster we humble ourselves and adjust to this change, the more effective we will be to shine as lights in the midst of a very dark time.

But for many who are unprepared, this day will overtake them like a thief in the night. I'm not talking about the third of the earth that will be destroyed. Those people will not know what hit them. Whoever that group is, this will be their last day.

The survivors will have to cope with all the changes. This day will steal everything that brought them life before, for the Lord has promised to take all of our idols away. Our luxurious lifestyles will be over, both sinners and saints.

Elementary Skills, Seeds of Hope, and a Strong Back

Communities of faith will survive the day; nothing else will. Lawlessness will break forth over all the earth. Faith communities can diffuse them and invite people into their shelter. There will always be plenty of room at the table in the kingdom of God. We will not hoard, but share. We will not curse, but bless. The kingdom will still continue on the earth as long as people of faith are here.

In these communities will be people with skills and knowledge. Computers won't be of any help, but a shovel and a hoe may save your life. We will need to grow our own food, can it for the long winters, hunt or herd our meat supplies, and butcher our own livestock. We will go back to the future. Only prepared hearts can be that abased and still maintain joy.

We will have to doctor our own and believe God for healing, because we won't be able to rely on modern medicine during these times. We will experience the same lives our ancestors knew. If we don't appreciate what we have now, we will then. All of the earth will be humbled.

If you want to save anything of value, then save seeds. In these seeds we have hope and can grow our own food. Seeds may be worth more than gold in the future.

We will have to work, or we will die. Perhaps the Lord will provide manna for us. I know that a lot of miracles will happen in this season, if we continue to believe and keep our faith. Yet it will be a difficult season of hard work for communities of faith. We must continue to care for the helpless and reach out to the dying. Our love will be tested and so will our backs! It will be hard work to till the ground by the sweat of our brow.

Be Strong, Act Like Men!

The Lord wants people who are willing to lay down their lives for each other. He doesn't want people focused on surviving—He calls us to serve. As long as I am still here, I want to be used of the Lord to harvest as many souls as I can and serve mankind in love.

The incessant focus on the early rapture of the church is, in essence, the wrong spirit. This focus is all about saving us from disaster, so we won't have to be here when things get hard. This teaching can grow into a bad doctrine, which wars against the truth of losing our lives for His sake. Jesus wants us to cultivate a spirit of laying down our lives for each other. The promises of Revelation are for him who overcomes and does not love his life unto death.

I Corinthians 16:13-14 says, "Be on the alert, stand firm in the faith, act like men, be strong. Let all that you do be done in love." I can't think of better advice for the end time church.

Will we all make it through the tribulation? No, I don't think so, just as I don't think that all believers who are alive today will be here seven years from now. But we can all make it to our destiny. If I have been placed here to give my life, then may I give it in service for Jesus. I am not even promised tomorrow, let alone to make it through the tribulation. How long I live should not be my goal. My goal should be to serve the Lord with all of my heart, faithfully, until my life is over.

What kind of person are you now? Whoever you are, it will be magnified in the end times. If you are a lover, then you will shine in the last days. If you are grateful, then you will be praising the Lord in the midst of the most difficult times on earth. If you have hope and joy, then people will ask you to give an account for the hope that is in you.

However, if you have hatred and bitterness, the venom that you spew out will wreak havoc. If you have fear, then fear will be your guide in these days. If you are hopeless or distressed, then your hopelessness will be contagious, and you will bring your family and community down to depression. The pressure of these days will bring out that which is hidden in our hearts.

INTERCESSORS AND PRAYERFUL PEOPLE

Who will survive the day of judgment? Only people who know how to depend on the Lord for everything they need. Jesus asked the question, "When the Son of Man comes, will He find faith on earth?" This question was asked in the context of prayer (Luke 18:7-8). Will God find people praying and crying out to Him day and night for justice and for help?

How will the Lord determine what regions of the earth will be saved and who will be destroyed on the day the thief is released? Some of this determination will happen because of our prayers. Intercessors, or the lack of them, always have determined the judgments of God.

When Sodom and Gomorrah was set for destruction, the Lord and Abraham debated over their judgment. In Genesis 18:16-33, Abraham interceded on their behalf. Because of his intercession, God offered to save these cities, had He found just ten righteous people. Even though ten could not be found, Lot and his family were saved and escorted out of the judgment zone. All of this happened because of Abraham's intercession.

The prophet Joel has given us the call to intercede for our cities and communities. He saw a people so aware of the coming judgment that even couples who were about to be married left their chambers to join in the fasting and weeping that was occurring before the altar of the Lord. Children were gathered, even nursing babes as the leaders declared this time of repentance. They all cried out, "Spare thy people, O Lord."

Do not underestimate prayer, repentance, and intercession. People who are going to the judgment are like sheep being led to the slaughter. They don't know what is going to befall them; intercessors do. They stand in the gap between heaven and earth and cry for deliverance. The Lord hears them; it is this cry that moves the heart of God.

Not only must we intercede before this day, we must be people of prayer to make it through the dark night when no man can work. We must ask the Lord for everything that we need, and trust Him completely during these days. There will be no other place to put our trust. Modern medicine will cease, stores will be no more, and every luxury that we have put our trust in will be destroyed. People who know their God, who prayerfully depend on Him, will make it through the night.

Do Not Fear
If there is one admonition that Jesus gave over and over again as He spoke about the last days of this age, it was not to fear. Fear will be the response of everyone who is unprepared for this day and will become a guiding emotion leading to more and more disaster as the tribulation unfolds.

Fear is a terrible guide and compass. When the world shakes, the people will be overcome with great fear. However, sprinkled all around them will be believers who were aware of this day and knew it was coming. Hopefully, they will have a much different reaction and response to the devastation of the day of the Lord.

As believers, we must view these coming days with faith and keep looking up, knowing that our redemption is drawing near. Jesus is doing all of this for us, and we must never lose focus of that during the last days, no matter how difficult they prove. Our faith will be tried and tested, but it will be found to be pure gold.

This hope within us will draw people to Jesus. Jesus told us specifically of these days so that we won't live in fear or react in fear. Preparation means everything. If this day takes us by surprise as well, then our reaction will be just like those who didn't see it coming or heed the warnings.

I know that I will probably be accused of bringing fear to the church because this book is not written from the perspective that we will all be raptured away before the terrible day of the Lord. My motives are exactly the opposite. If we don't prepare for this day, we will all be taken off guard and perish in our fear. When I know that something is going to happen, it takes the sudden surprise away and allows me to be proactive in preparation for the day. I desire nothing more for the church to wake up to the reality of what these last days hold for all men. This terrible day of the Lord is not to be longed for, but to be prepared for. All of the New Testament was given to prepare us for this day.

If this is the first time you have studied the day of the Lord, welcome to a new understanding of the most prophesied day in the Bible. If you are living immorally or are in love with this world, then repent and turn to Jesus. I promise you it is not too late. There is still room at the table of the kingdom of Jesus. Come.

The day of the Lord is both a great and terrible day. First, it will be terrible. Its one purpose is to judge this present Babylonian system of nations, idolatry, immorality, and religions. Its goal is to vanquish this Babylonian system and establish the kingdom of Jesus on the earth. The terrible day is sent as a response to the blood of all the righteous saints who have given their lives in service to their King. It will be a wrathful day, but the bride of Christ is going to make herself ready during these difficult times. She will be brave and do mighty exploits during these last days. Jesus, who is in her, will shine brightly in the end.

Then, the great day of the Lord will come, when Jesus will return to earth, gather His saints, vanquish His enemies, and establish His rule and reign on the earth. Out of Zion, Jesus will rule, and the entire earth will be filled with the knowledge of the Lord and the peace of His kingdom. The earth will be restored, and the saints will rule this earth with imperishable bodies given to us at the resurrection of the saints.

Are you ready for what is soon to come upon the entire earth? How late is the hour? Keep watching Israel, for she is certainly in the center of God's plans for these end times. The war of words between Israel and Iran may soon escalate into the very situation that causes Ezekiel 38 to come to pass.

I can't tell you when the day of the Lord will arrive, or where to go to escape, but I can admonish you to listen and prepare. The Judge is at the door, being held back for the day and hour of his release. At some point in the very near future, the thief will be released with vengeance. May God have mercy on the souls of this generation.

Are there any scriptures yet unfulfilled as we await the arrival of the thief? I do not claim to be a prophecy expert, but I don't see anything prophetically standing in the way of the thief. Every type of birth pang that Jesus foretold has arrived, but perhaps they will increase with more intensity and frequency. That is not a pleasant thought either. My sense is that the birth pangs will begin to intensify very soon.

Are you prepared? Are you alert in prayer, sensitive to the voice of Jesus, growing in love and obedience to our Lord Jesus Christ? Are you ready, truly ready for the Lord's soon return? Is mankind ready for the most difficult season that they have ever faced in history? I don't think so.

So let's warn them. Let us at least love them enough to tell them the truth about the day that we know is just around the corner. Share this book with them and ask them their thoughts. Ask them if they know Jesus; are they sure of their destiny? Let us lead as many as we can safely into the shelter of the Most High before it is too late.

Jesus clearly taught us that the one who endures until the end will be saved (Matthew 24:13). Our end may be death, but our testimony will remain strong. I honestly don't know which will be easier, to suffer death or to remain on and experience everything that leads up to the coming of the Lord. It will not be easy to be faithful, no matter what befalls us. "And unless those days had been cut short, no life would have been saved; but for the sake of the elect, those days shall be cut short (Matthew 24:22)."

Our hope is Jesus Christ, and His return to this earth. With every birth pang of judgment, our redemption draws nearer. So let us continue to gather together and stimulate one another to love, to serve, and to be faithful. Let us wholeheartedly trust in Jesus to deliver us from evil and set us securely in His kingdom. And most of all, let us fulfill the Great Commission with hearts that passionately love our neighbors, proclaiming to them the Great King who is returning, and warning them of the purifying judgment that awaits mankind.

Has the revelation of the bride emerging during the tribulation, instead of being rescued from it, given you a fresh perspective of the end times? It is one thing to think that horrible things will happen after we are gone; it is quite another to see ourselves in the same fire.

My only desire is for all of us to wake up and be about the Lord's business faithfully, until He returns. I pray that you are much more sober and realize just how short our time is to fulfill this season of the times of the Gentiles. May God richly bless and empower you as a harvester in these last days.

"Now to Him who is able to keep you from stumbling, and to make you stand in the presence of His glory, blameless, with great joy, to the only God our Savior through Jesus Christ our Lord, be glory, majesty, dominion, and authority before all time, now and forever. Amen."

The Ten Undeniable Facts of the Day of the Lord

1. This day began when Jesus was born on earth. His life, teaching, restoration ministry, substitutionary death, resurrection, ascension, and founding His church completed His first mission to the earth.

2. Jesus ruled over the history of man since His ascension, from the throne of heaven seated at the right hand of the Father, until His enemies are made a footstool for His feet. He also has been our Great High Priest, interceding for us at the right hand of the Father.

3. Israel was and will be regathered to the land that God gave them. Though she will not be totally expelled from this land, neither will Israel go unpunished during the purifying judgment.

4. Nations will be warned of the coming day of the Lord by birth pangs, which are intermittent short judgments that will cause dismay in these nations.

5. The terrible day of the Lord will come like a thief in the night with severe intensity. This day will begin the last day's judgment of the world. The Bible predicts that Israel will be saved from the disaster of this day.

6. The antichrist will arise again and trouble Israel. He will gather nations together to destroy Jerusalem, but all their armies will be destroyed on the day Jesus returns. This judg-

ment ends this present age and the tribulation season of the day of the Lord.

7. Jesus returns with His saints who are gathered and resurrected to join Him for the marriage supper of the Lamb, the battle that vanquishes their enemies.

8. Jesus will rule from Jerusalem in the temple that He builds, and all nations will be subject to Him. His saints will join Him in ruling the earth.

9. His judgments will include no more war, animals will graze together and no longer harm; the lame, blind, deaf, and dumb will be healed. An early bema seat judgment for the saints, and a later judgment of the nations are also included in His earthly judgments.

10. Satan will be released and gather the rebellious for a war in his final stand on the earth. As earlier decreed by Jesus, there will be no war, as fire falls from heaven and consumes them all. This event will culminate the day of the Lord. A new age will begin.

THE DAY

About the Author

Jim Thomas has a teaching ministry in Salisbury, North Carolina. He has been a pastor for more than thirty years, most of them in a small Mennonite community in southwest Pennsylvania. Jim is a husband of thirty-five years, father of two young men, and grandfather of four.

Jim is the author of three other books:
    The Place—Experience the Journey to Where God Dwells
        (First Light Ministries)
    Road to Royalty—Seven Stages of Growth in the Life of a
        Christian (Pleasant Word)
    BC—The Blessing and the Curse (Noah's Ark Publishing)
His passion for the Word of God is evident in his writing and in his teaching ministry.

If you would like to contact Jim for seminar teachings or for any speaking engagements, contact:

First Light Ministries
1255 West Ridge Road
Salisbury, NC 28147

THE DAY

Made in the USA
Charleston, SC
29 November 2012